LETTING FRENCH PROPERTY SUCCESSFULLY

Stephen Smith and Charles Parkinson

LETTING FRENCH PROPERTY SUCCESSFULLY

Letting French Property Successfully

© *Stephen Smith and Charles Parkinson*

ISBN 0-9543490-0-8

A CIP catalogue record of this book is available from the British Library.

Published by:
PKF (Guernsey) Limited
PO Box 296, St Peter Port, Guernsey GY1 4NA
Telephone: 01481 727927. Facsimile: 01481 710511

Typeset and design by PKF (Guernsey) Ltd
and Avonset, Bath
Printed in Great Britain by Cromwell Press Ltd, Trowbridge, Wiltshire
Fourth Edition

Disclaimer

The information contained in this book is offered as a basis for further consideration only and is not to be acted upon without independent advice from suitably qualified professionals based on the actual circumstances of the taxpayer.

Neither the publisher nor the author can accept any responsibility for any loss occasioned to any person no matter howsoever caused or arising as a result of or in consequence of action taken or refrained from in reliance on the contents of this book.

WHERE TO GO FOR FURTHER ADVICE AND INFORMATION

Although all the main issues are considered in this book, it is impossible to discuss every subject in detail within this format and this book should not therefore be considered as exhaustive and sufficient in itself to make investment decisions. Professional advice should be sought in connection with specific cases and the issues arising from them. Neither the publisher nor the authors can accept any responsibility for any loss occasioned to any person no matter howsoever caused or arising as a result of or in consequence of action taken or refrained from in reliance on the contents of this book.

If you would like more advice or information on French property and related matters, please contact **Stephen Smith** at:

> **Stephen Smith (France) Ltd**
> 161 Cemetery Road,
> Ipswich,
> Suffolk IP4 2HL
> Tel: (01473) 437186
> Fax: (01473) 436573
> Email: stephen@stephensmithfranceltd.com
> Website: www.stephensmithfranceltd.com
> (International dialling code: 44 1473)

For further information on French tax and related matters, please contact **Charles Parkinson, Virginie Deflassieux** or **Kate Brehaut** at:

> **PKF (Guernsey) Ltd**
> P O Box 296
> St Peter Port
> Guernsey GY1 4NA
> Tel: (01481) 727927
> Fax: (01481) 710511
> Email: french.tax@pkfguernsey.com
> Website: pkfguernsey.com
> (International dialling code: 44 1481)

Also available from PKF (Guernsey) Ltd:
'Taxation in France', by Charles Parkinson
'Taxation in Spain', by Andrew Hall

CONTENTS

Page

Introduction   **viii**

1.   Practical considerations   **1**
1.1   Choosing the location   1
1.2   Choosing the property   2
1.3   Budgeting   2
         1.3.1   Purchase and ownership costs   2
         1.3.2   Local taxes   3
         1.3.3   Other outgoings   4
1.4   Raising finance   4

2.   The purchase process and ownership structuring   **5**
2.1   The importance of taking early independent advice   5
2.2   Conveyancing   6
2.3   Buying a new property   7
         2.3.1   The contract   7
         2.3.2   Completion   8
2.4   Buying a flat   9
2.5   'Leaseback' purchases   10
2.6   Structuring your ownership   12
         2.6.1   Ownership as individuals   12
         2.6.2   French succession law and inheritance tax   13
         2.6.3   Ownership of French property via a company   17
                 a)   Offshore companies   17
                 b)   Ownership of French property via an SCI   18
                 c)   Other companies   19
         2.6.4   Ownership via trusts   19

3.   Making the property lettable   **20**
3.1   Renovation and conversion   20
3.2   Furniture   21
3.3   Linen   21
3.4   Kitchen equipment   21
3.5   Domestic equipment   21
3.6   Cleaning, maintenance, caretaking and receiving guests   22
3.7   Insurance and safety   22

4.	**Marketing and management**	**24**
4.1	Brochures	24
4.2	Where to advertise	24
4.3	Letting and managing agents	25
5.	**Letting agreements**	**27**
5.1	Short-term lets of furnished property	27
	5.1.1 The landlord's main obligations	28
	5.1.2 The tenant's main obligations	28
5.2	Contents of a short-term letting agreement	29
5.3	Letting furnished property for more than six months	31
5.4	Letting unfurnished property in France	31
5.5	Letting land	31
6.	**Letting as a business**	**33**
6.1	French transfer duty	33
6.2	Structuring the investment	33
	6.2.1 The property	34
	6.2.2 The business	34
	6.2.3 French commercial companies	35
6.3	Running a business in France	36
	6.3.1 Planning permission	37
	6.3.2 Sale or supply of alcohol	37
	6.3.3 Restaurants and hotels	38
	6.3.4 Employment law and social security	38
7.	**Taxation**	**39**
7.1	Taxation of rental income from the property owned by non-residents	39
	7.1.1 Self declaration	39
	7.1.2 Penalties for late payment or filing incorrect returns	39
7.2	Basis of assessment	40
	7.2.1 Residence	40
	7.2.2 Unfurnished property	41
	7.2.3 Furnished property	42
	7.2.4 Deductible expenses	43
	7.2.5 Business asset	44
	7.2.6 Choosing the right basis of assessment	44
7.3	Other French taxes	45
	7.3.1 TVA	45
	7.3.2 Taxe professionnelle	46
	7.3.3 Tax on leases	46

		Page
7.4	French corporation tax	47
7.5	Taxation of property speculators	48
7.6	Liability to tax in the UK	48

APPENDIX A: PRECEDENTS   **49**

Preface			49
	a)	Language	49
	b)	Jurisdiction	49
	c)	Law	50
A.1		English language agreement made subject mainly to the jurisdiction of the courts of England and Wales	50
A.2		French language holiday letting agreement made subject to the jurisdiction of the French courts and to French law	56
A.3		French furnished letting agreement for a duration of 6 months or longer	64

APPENDIX B: Typical Income Tax Computations   **84**

APPENDIX C: French-English Glossary for Home Buyers and Home Owners   **87**

INTRODUCTION

In recent years, thousands of UK families or groups of friends have bought a property in France to escape from cold winters and wet summers. For many, their personal use of the property is a source of considerable pleasure. Although by British standards property prices in France are still generally low, and purchase loans are readily available, many potential buyers are discouraged from purchasing French property for two main reasons. Firstly, they do not want to feel tied down to the same property each year when there are other countries or parts of France to explore. Secondly, their available holiday time is often limited to two or three weeks in the summer and, although friends and relatives may occasionally visit the property, it will otherwise remain unoccupied for the rest of the year.

On the other hand, more than 25 million tourists visit France each year. This is not a passing phenomenon and with new, improved and cheaper transport links, the demand for self-catering accommodation in France continues to grow from foreign holidaymakers, especially in Britain and northern Europe.

The purpose of this book is to provide a guide to the main practical, legal and tax processes necessary to let your property successfully in France. It reflects the current laws as at 31 July 2002 and explains how, in the short term, the rent you charge might not only cover annual maintenance and other expenses, but also leave you with surplus income to pay for your own holiday. With careful planning, more systematic lettings could also earn you enough income to recover your initial capital outlay and borrowings. You may even decide to buy more property to let as a business!

1.   PRACTICAL CONSIDERATIONS

1.1   CHOOSING THE LOCATION

Although landlords ('you') and your tenants will be welcome in most *communes*, many properties in France have no letting potential. As a landlord, your choice of property should be dictated by what your tenants are likely to want. For example, a converted barn in a beautiful, peaceful but remote part of France is less likely to attract regular tenants than a well-furnished property which is within fairly easy reach of shops, restaurants and other tourist attractions.

Under the French Planning Code, properties located in Paris, within 50 kilometres of 'ancient Parisian fortifications' and in *communes* with a population of at least 10,000 inhabitants cannot be converted into furnished lettings if the landlord is classed as a 'professional' (see 7.2.5). Some other *communes* in France have voluntarily adopted the same restriction and the position should always therefore be carefully checked if you are intending to let furnished property in France as a 'professional'. However, the French Planning Code states that this restriction will not apply to properties in areas of France which are 'habitually let out in the holiday season' (eg seaside, ski or spa resorts).

The tourist industry in some parts of France is estimated to have dropped by up to 30% in recent years. Most *départements* have a tourist office whose English-speaking staff can supply information free of charge on all aspects of tourism within their region. The French Government Tourist Board in London (Tel: 09068 244123) may also be able to help.

Demand for properties starts earliest in coastal parts of France, especially the Vendée and Charente Maritime; followed by Normandy and Brittany, Provence and Languedoc-Roussillon. The season for inland regions start a little later.

Inland regions tend to experience extremes of temperature with hot summers and freezing winters, whereas north of the Loire valley and along the Atlantic coast, the climate is similar to Britain. Many tourists are drawn to the south and (cheaper) south-west regions of France which usually enjoy hot dry periods lasting unbroken from early spring till late autumn, and cool dry winters. First choice is usually for properties with private swimming pools. The investment return in a swimming pool can be recovered in a very short time.

Apart from climatic factors, distance and ease of travel are important considerations. Properties in Brittany and Normandy are often in demand because tenants (especially those with young families) can reach them without travelling long distances. There is no doubt that the Channel Tunnel has made access to North-Eastern France and the main *autoroutes* to the South much easier. Many properties are also within easy reach of a daily air, rail or motorail connection, although some services do not operate at weekends, or only operate in the summer. Whatever the weather, many properties located in the mountains or close to ski resorts have an all year-round letting potential.

1.2 CHOOSING THE PROPERTY

Although a newly-built property is generally easier and cheaper to maintain, an older property which has been well modernised and equipped is more likely to appeal to tenants.

A local French estate agent (*agent immobilier*) or letting agent (*agent de location*) may, without charge or obligation, help you find a property with letting potential and advise on the likely rent that may be achieved. French estate agents will not usually supply a list of properties for sale and their particulars tend to be brief and handwritten without a colour photograph or room dimensions. Money can be saved and fruitless visits avoided by instructing a recommended British agent specialising in French property to help you find a suitable property in your chosen region of France.

If you own a flat, villa or other property forming part of a larger development, the *règlement de copropriété* or internal regulations should be checked to ensure that there are no restrictions on your ability to let the property. In some cases, you must obtain written consent to let the property from the *syndic* or managing agent of the development. Even if there are no restrictions on letting, it is always prudent for insurance reasons to supply the *syndic* with written details of the periods when the property will be occupied and by whom.

The letting agreement should oblige the tenant to observe all the internal regulations and he should therefore be supplied with a copy of the relevant parts of the *règlement de copropriété* (with an English-language translation if necessary) before he takes occupation.

1.3 BUDGETING

You should budget for legal and survey fees; annual taxes and outgoings; transport costs to and from the property, furniture, maintenance and renovation expenses.

1.3.1 Purchase and ownership costs

Your vendor will normally pay the estate agent's commission, but it is customary for the buyer to pay the legal fees and duties relating to the purchase. The legal fees charged by a *Notaire* or French property lawyer are currently calculated as follows:

Bands	%
€0 to €3,050	5
€3,050 to €6,100	3.3
€6,100 to €16,770	1.65
€16,770 upwards	0.825

French VAT ('TVA') at 19.6% is paid on the purchase of a new property. A sale of a building will be subject to TVA either if the property is sold before it is completed; or if it is sold within 5 years of its completion, not having previously been sold by a non-trader. When the property acquired is less than 5 years old, TVA is paid by the vendor, but in practice this means that it is added to the sale price.

If the property is more than 5 years old, no TVA is payable, but the transaction is subject to stamp duties (*droits d'enregistrement*). The element of this tax paid to the *département* is currently set around 3.6%. In addition, an element of 1.2% is paid to the local *commune*. In all, stamp duties total 4.8% and are payable by the purchaser unless the parties agree otherwise.

When a building plot is acquired (or the property consists of buildings to be demolished to make way for new construction) the purchase is subject to TVA at the normal rate – which is usually borne by the purchaser. The transfer is also subject to a 'publicity tax' of 0.6% based on the net of TVA value. Work performed by building contractors is normally subject to TVA at 19.6%. In larger communities there may be an additional building tax of between 1 and 5%.

Certain improvement, transformation, or maintenance works carried out on residential property over two years old may be subject to a reduced TVA rate of 5.5%. This TVA reduction applies until 31 December 2002 (unless it is extended).

1.3.2 Local taxes

The *taxes foncières* or local land and property taxes are levied on the owner of French property each year, calculated by reference to its theoretical rental value set by the local *cadastre* or land registry. New or renovated properties are generally exempt from these taxes for 2 years commencing on 1 January following the date of their structural completion, provided the work undertaken has been declared within 90 days of its completion. A *taxe d'habitation* charge is also payable each year by the occupier (owner or tenant) of any property suitable for residential occupation. If the letting is seasonal, the owner is more likely to pay the *taxe d'habitation*. In some parts of France, sundry taxes or *taxes assimilées* will also be charged by the local authority for the supply of snow sweeping or other amenities. These taxes are usually lower than similar charges in the UK.

When a property is transfered, the vendor usually pays the *taxe d'habitation* due in respect of the year of transfer. However the *taxes foncières* is usually split between the vendor and the purchaser on a pro-rata temporis basis.

1.3.3 Other outgoings

You will be responsible for the cost of electricity, gas, water, telephone and other supplies from the date of completion of your purchase. If you own a flat, you will also be liable for the cost of annual maintenance and service charges. You should also budget for compulsory buildings and contents insurance premiums (see 3.7).

1.4 RAISING FINANCE

There are two ways in which you can raise finance to purchase residential property in France. The most popular way is to borrow in French Francs from a French bank or other lender. As a general rule, French lenders will allow you to borrow up to 80% of the purchase price and improvement costs over a term of between 5 and 15 years. The loan will not usually include mortgage arrangement fees, legal fees and attendant purchase expenses. Monthly repayments are usually made by direct debit from a French bank account which you will be asked to open prior to completing the loan. Life assurance cover is usually also required. If you need to borrow money to improve or renovate the property, it is advisable to apply for a mortgage before you buy the property as French banks will not always lend you the necessary funds once you own the property.

If you take out a loan on the security of a French property, a further registration fee of between 1% and 2% of the monies borrowed will be charged and it may therefore be more cost effective to borrow from a financial institution in your own country by creating a charge over or remortgaging your main residence, or offering other assets as security for the loan.

When applying for a loan, some banks will ask you for a cash flow forecast detailing anticipated capital and income expenses and the rental income you expect to earn.

If the property is mortgaged, it is essential that written permission for the letting is obtained from the building society or bank which granted the mortgage. They may have a standard form of notice which will have to be signed by both the landlord and the prospective tenant. The building society or bank may also charge a higher rate of interest as the letting may be regarded as a commercial arrangement.

2. THE PURCHASE PROCESS AND OWNERSHIP STRUCTURING

2.1 THE IMPORTANCE OF TAKING EARLY INDEPENDENT PROFESSIONAL ADVICE

French estate agents often invite you to sign their own pre-printed contract. It is very important not to sign anything without legal advice. Some contracts bear English translations, but many are misleading or unintelligible. Having French documents translated into English is not enough. The contract should also be checked to establish whether, in addition to the purchase price, you will also be liable to pay the estate agent's commission. What has been left out of a French document can be just as important as its contents. Once you have signed a contract, you are almost always bound to complete the purchase. Before signing a contract, you should therefore ensure that it truly records what you have agreed and contains all the appropriate clauses for your protection. If not, you lose the opportunity to insert your own tailor-made requirements. If a dispute arises, you must instruct an *avocat* or barrister specialising in contentious work. Many foreign purchasers have found themselves involved in expensive legal proceedings in France because they were unable or unwilling to complete a transaction and were not fully aware of the terms of their contract.

Transfers of real property (land and buildings) in France have to be witnessed by a public official called a *Notaire*. In some cases, the *Notaire* also acts as an estate agent, and may have drawn up the contract, but it is not usual for him to be involved until after you have signed the contract and become legally bound to buy a property. The *Notaire* is often instructed to act for both the vendor and the purchaser. A purchaser has the right to choose his own separate *Notaire* and should not usually instruct the *Notaire* acting for the seller. Unlike a Solicitor, the *Notaire* is not appointed to represent your interests but acts as an intermediary for both parties to a French property transaction. As an independent official, his main duty of care is to ensure that the documents which legally transfer ownership of the property are in order. *Notaires* do not usually regard it as necessary to keep you informed about your purchase or mortgage application. They will not perform the role or give you the same security and protection as you would expect from an English Solicitor. Questions on many aspects of your transaction cannot be answered by lawyers and other professionals in France since they involve considerations of foreign law. For example, what happens to your English property if you die in France? Who pays what taxes, and to which country?

You should therefore approach every aspect of your French purchase with caution and seek proper advice at the earliest stages from bilingual lawyers in your home country who have the knowledge and experience to liaise with the *Notaire* by telephone or fax when the need arises and to advise on both French law and the interplay of French and English (or other foreign) law.

2.2   CONVEYANCING

French law does not recognise the concept of 'subject to contract' and, once you have chosen a property and agreed a purchase price, according to Article 1583 of the French Civil Code you have entered into a binding contract. In practice, you will be asked to sign a preliminary contract at this early stage. Before you make any legal commitment, you should consider obtaining a structural survey report and valuation. Your vendor does not usually have to disclose any structural defects affecting the property. This means that if, after signing a contract, you discover structural or other defects to the property and its equipment/services, you are still obliged to complete the purchase at the agreed price and cannot obtain compensation from your vendor.

You should also obtain an up-to-date registered plan or *plan cadastral* of the property which shows the extent and boundaries of the property. Legal advice should be taken if this is not clear. It is prudent to check the legal title and other documents for rights of way and other easements which might adversely affect your enjoyment of the property, and whether planning permission or some other consent was/will be required for any construction or change to the external aspect or permitted user of the property. Planning permission (see 3.1) is sometimes required if you want to install a swimming pool, septic tank, or improvement works to the interior of the property. The property or the area in which it is situated may be protected in some way, in which case it is an offence to make any alterations or improvements without first obtaining a special type of planning permission. There may be other matters which, although not visible, could adversely affect your use and enjoyment of the property. In every case, proper enquiries and searches should be made.

There are two main forms of contract. The more common type is a *compromis de vente* which is an agreement signed by both parties and subsequently reiterated before the *Notaire* by a deed of sale called an *acte de vente*. In some parts of France, the transaction is recorded in a one-sided document called a *promesse de vente*. Whatever the type of contract used, it should not be signed before you have had it thoroughly checked and approved.

When the contract has been signed by the buyer a deposit of 10% of the purchase price is payable. If the property is less than 5 years old the deposit will be 5%. This is deposited with the *Notaire* witnessing the conveyance, or the estate agent if he is authorised to accept deposits. The deposit is a part payment of the purchase price if the contract is completed, but it is forfeited if the buyer withdraws from the contract, and the seller must usually pay the buyer the same amount in damages (as well as refunding the deposit) if he withdraws from the contract. The contract will usually contain conditions, such as that it is subject to the buyer obtaining finance; if these conditions are not fulfilled the deposit is refundable. Because of the penalty of the amount of the deposit, it is rare to see sellers breaking a sale agreement to accept a higher offer.

Once the conveyancing documents have been completed by the *Notaire*, normally after 4-8 weeks, the buyer is asked to pay to the *Notaire* the balance of the purchase price. The *Notaire* is personally liable for the registration taxes on the sale and will also insist on having these and his costs before proceeding. The buyer and seller have to be present before the *Notaire*, in person or by giving a Power of Attorney, for the signature of the *acte de vente*.

If the property to be acquired is unfinished, the parties will sign a reservation contract and the purchaser will pay a deposit of 5% if the property is to be completed within a year, 2% if the property is to be completed within 1-2 years and no deposit if the property will be completed after more than 2 years.

2.3   BUYING A NEW PROPERTY IN FRANCE

If you buy a new flat, villa or other property (under construction or less than 5 years old) forming part of a larger development in France, the *Code de la Construction et de l'Habitation* should protect you if the developer goes bankrupt, or from other possible pitfalls.

2.3.1   The Contract

When you have decided on a property and agreed a price, the developer will – at an early stage – ask you to sign a *contrat de réservation* or *contrat préliminaire* (all other types of contract are void) and to pay a *réservation* (non-interest bearing deposit). If the building works are to be completed within one year of signing the contract, the deposit cannot exceed 5% (2% if within two years; no deposit if longer). The contract should – but often does not – provide:

a) A full description and the approximate *surface habitable* of the *partie privative*;

b) A layout plan (*plan de masse*) and a floor plan (*plan des locaux*) of the *partie privative*;

c) A specification note (*notice technique sommaire*) giving details of the building materials and domestic services and fittings to be provided. It is important that you fully understand this technical document to avoid any disappointment at a later stage when it would be difficult to change the specifications;

d) If the purchase price is firm and final (in some cases the developer can increase it);

e) The date by which the building works will have to be completed. A financial guarantee must be provided, either by the developer (*garantie intrinsèque*) or by a third party (*garantie extrinsèque*). A prudent buyer will ensure that the latter is obtained. The third party guarantor must be an accredited financial institution that will arrange for the completion of building works or the refund of the purchase price in the event of the developer's failure to complete;

f) Any *conditions suspensives* (special conditions) you wish to add to the contract.

As explained in section 2.4 below, you should not sign the contract without having seen and studied the *réglement de copropriété* and the *état descriptif de division* (both technical documents) and have a good idea of the amount of annual maintenance and service charges you will have to pay.

A copy of the signed contract must be given to you before you make any payments. If you do not sign the contract in from of a *notaire,* it will only become legally binding seven days after you have received a copy of the contract by registered letter which can be proved by acknowledgement of receipt ('LRAR'). In this time, you may usually withdraw from the contract if you serve written notice on the developer by LRAR. Any complaints you may have throughout the building programme should also be sent to the developer by fax and/or LRAR.

2.3.2 Completion

You will eventually receive a statutory notice asking you to complete the purchase, together with a draft (*project*) of the *acte de vente* (transfer deed).

You complete your purchase by signing the transfer deed which conveys ownership to you of the – usually incompleted – *partie privative* and *parties communes*. You automatically acquire ownership of the rest of your property – for which you pay installments of the purchase price – as the building works progress. Stage payments are usually made as follows:

–   35% on completion of the foundations;

–   35% on the building being made watertight;

–   25% on completion of the building.

When the property is fit for occupation, you will be asked for the last stage payment. Provided the building work is generally completed as specified in the contract, then you must accept it. Only a substantial defect would entitle you to withhold the last payment. French law allows a reasonable delay for completion of landscaping and other ancillary works.

From the day the keys are handed over, there is a one-month guarantee period against visible structural defects. French law also provides you with a 10-year warranty against latent defects which affect the structure of the building including those resulting from subsoil conditions. All those involved in the building programme may be liable unless it can be proved that the damage was caused by something outside their control. There is also a 2-year warranty against defects in equipment (e.g. central heating) in the building.

Whilst France sets a high standard for the protection of purchasers of new property, there are still many pitfalls. To avoid these, it is essential to take proper advice at an early stage of your purchase from someone will versed in the legal technicalities involved.

2.4   BUYING A FLAT

There are many advantages (and rental income opportunities) to owning a French flat which, in holiday resorts or cities, is often the most affordable option.

As a *copropriétaire*, you do not buy a lease in a development but own the freehold to (a) the *partie privative* – flat, storage room, garage etc., designated for you exclusive use – and; (b) a share of the *parties communes* – staircases, lifts, gardens, swimming pool etc., - for which all *copropriétaires* (who are jointly responsible for their maintenance and upkeep) must pay service charges.

By signing the French purchase contract, you are legally bound by the *règlement de copropriété* ('RDC') which contains all the rules and your liabilities relating to the management, upkeep and appearance of the development. You should therefore insist on having sight of a full registered copy of this important document before you commit yourself to a purchase. Even if you speak fluent French, you are unlikely to understand this technical document without bilingual legal assistance.

The RDC contains a detailed description of your property, stipulating which parts are private and which are common (balconies and other parts of a development can be either). Generally, *copropriétaires* can only use their *partie privative* for private residential – i.e. non-commercial – purposes. The position should however always be checked. There are cases of buyers taking flats near property which, although originally residential in user, became fishmongers, nightclubs or other similar nuisances.

The RDC also provides 'house rules' and regulates the permitted external appearance of your property (e.g. blinds, exterior paintwork and drying clothes on balconies). There will be restrictions on where you or your guests can park cars. The French courts may modify the provisions of an RDC which are unreasonably restrictive or unfair.

All *copropriétaires* automatically and compulsorily become members of a *syndicat* which is responsible for the development. Usually, a *syndic* (professional manager) is appointed to be responsible for the day-to-day running of the development. He is often assisted in a consultative capacity by a management committee (*conseil syndical*) comprised of *copropriétaires*.

An annual general meeting must be held to approve the accounts for the previous year and to prepare a budget for the next year (if an important matter arises, an extraordinary general meeting can be convened). In both cases, 15 days' notice must be given together with the agenda. All *copropriétaires* can attend meetings which are held in French, and difficult to understand.

If voting rules have been properly followed, adopted resolutions are binding on all *copropriétaires*. The law specifies which type of voting must be used for different matters, e.g:

-   simple majority for approval of annual accounts and budgets;

-   absolute majority for appointment and dismissal of the *syndic*;

-   unanimity for change of user and modification of allocation of service charges.

The insurance of the common parts of the development is the responsibility of the *copropriété* as a whole and is usually delegated to the *syndic*. The premiums will form part of the annual service charge made for the maintenance of the building. The insurance of the *partie privative* is the responsibility of each *copropriétaire*. It is an offence not to have minimum third party civil liability insurance by the date of completion. However, it is essential to consult the *syndic* before taking out insurance as it is becoming more and more common for *copropriétés* to effect insurance in respect of both the common and private parts of the development.

If you are thinking of letting your property, the RDC should be checked to ensure that there are no restrictions. In some cases, you must obtain written consent from the *syndic* to let your property. Even if there are no restrictions on letting, it is always prudent for insurance reasons to supply the *syndic* with written details of the periods when the property will be occupied and by whom.

Your (written) letting agreement should oblige the tenant to observe all the regulations and he should therefore be supplied with a copy of the relevant parts of the RDC (with an English language translation if necessary) before he takes occupation.

2.5   'LEASEBACK' PURCHASES

In some new French property developments, the developer offers a reduction in the purchase price of up to 40% in exchange for the purchaser leasing the property back to the developer for most of the year. The VAT on the purchase price may also be refunded to the investor in such cases, resulting in a considerable saving on the total price. A further benefit of a purchase structured in this way is that the purchaser is deemed to have paid the full price (net of VAT if this has been refunded), and his future capital gain therefore does not include the discount given to him by the developer.

The developer will let the property to tourists for the majority of the year, and the buyer retains the right to occupy the property rent-free for (usually) up to 6 weeks a year. The buyer may receive part of the rental income, depending on the terms of the agreement (and in particular on the level of discount the developer has given in the purchase price).

The conditions that must be fulfilled so that this apparently attractive arrangement achieves the desired fiscal and practical results are listed below, it being assumed, as will nearly always be the case, that the buyer has purchased a flat:

a) The flat must be in a building which is 'classé'. This means that it has to the satisfaction of the Préfet of the département in which it is situated complied with the regulations relating to properties let to tourists ('résidences de tourisme').

b) The lease must be for at least 9 years. In addition at least 70% of the flats in the same building must be similarly let.

c) The letting must be for the purposes of 'exploitation para-hôtelière' (the provision of hotel-like services) since lettings of property with no provision of food are exempt from VAT, and the buyer would not then get his VAT refund.

d) The management company must undertake to promote French tourism abroad. In addition, during the first 2 years it must undertake to spend at least 1.5% of the income from the sub-lettings on seeking foreign tourists, or it must enter into contracts with tourist agencies to put at their disposal at least 20% of the available letting space.

e) The management company will be required to keep the premises and its contents in a good state of repair and fully insured and to pay all taxes which would normally fall on a tenant. The buyer/landlord covenants to pay the service charges and taxes normally paid by an owner (including the taxes foncières and the taxe d'habitation) and to pay the management company a sum for its services.

f) The management company pays rent at two rates, depending on whether the buyer is in occupation or not. The rent is linked to what the management company receives from its sub-lettings, and is usually paid annually in arrears.

At the end of the contract, the buyer is supposed to obtain vacant possession, however under French law the management company, as the lessee, has the right to the renewal of the lease. If the renewal is not granted, the tenant has a right to compensation. Since this does not form any part of the intentions of the parties at the outset, some management companies offer to indemnify the owner or to procure the indemnity of another company in their group in an amount equal to the amount to which the management company would be entitled on a refusal of a renewal. The difficulty is of course that the company providing the indemnity may have gone out of business in 9 year's time. The solution is to get the management company to execute a waiver of its rights (which cannot be done in the lease itself or at the same time as the lease is executed, so the buyer will be at risk for a short period). The buyer/landlord must also insist on the introduction of a clause into the lease prohibiting assignments of the lease without the consent of the landlord and requiring that the landlord is a party to any assignment so that he can impose the effect of the waiver on the assignee.

2.6   STRUCTURING YOUR OWNERSHIP

In many cases a non-resident buying property in France will be buying it jointly with his or her spouse, or in partnership with other non-residents. The purchasers will therefore be keen to arrange their ownership so that they each have appropriate rights to the property, particularly in the event of one of the co-owners dying. In the French tax system, individuals owning French property who are 'domiciled' (i.e. habitually resident) abroad are generally treated more favourably than companies which own property in France. However, as explained below, it may not be appropriate for you to own French property as individuals.

2.6.1   *Ownership as individuals*

The main forms of joint ownership are *indivision* and *tontine*. In practical terms, the difference is that when property is owned by two or more individuals *en indivision*, and one of them dies, his or her share devolves to his or her heirs under the rules of French succession law (see below). When property is owned *en tontine*, the survivor of the owners is deemed to have owned the whole property from the beginning.

An *indivision* can simply result from a succession.

In France, a deceased's assets do not pass to Executors (who distribute them in accordance with his Will), but immediately vest in his *réserve* and other beneficiaries *en indivision*; and the administration of the estate is in their hands. This can lead to serious family squabbles.

For example, if an *indivisaire* (co-owner *en indivision*) wants to sell his share of a French house to an outsider, he must give written notice to the other *indivisaire* (s) who can themselves purchase that share in place of the outsider. If an *indivisaire* cannot sell his share (at the price he wants) to the other *indivisaires* or to an outsider, the French courts can order that the whole of the property be sold without the consent of the other *indivisaires*. To avoid the above and other possible problems, *indivisaires* can enter into a binding *convention d'indivision* which regulates the use, management and devolution of the property.

However, a *convention* cannot avoid the following possible problem. If on an *indivisaire's* death one or more of his children is under 18 years of age (or any of his children have predeceased him leaving minor issue), the deceased's surviving spouse or other *indivisaire (s)* may not be able to sell or otherwise dispose of the property until the youngest of any minors reaches the age of majority. This is because minors cannot themselves sell French *immeubles*. If the minors are French domiciled, the French courts can in some cases authorise a surviving parent or other person to dispose of the minors' property in France. If the minors are domiciled in England, the French courts have no jurisdiction, and under English law the English courts cannot authorise a surviving parent, trustee or guardian to dispose of the minor's French property.

Most *notaires* issue no warning to English buyers about the problems of owning French property *en indivision*, which can usually be avoided or mitigated in a number of ways by taking advice from lawyers well versed in the laws of both countries, preferably before you acquire French property.

For example, it costs nothing to insert a *tontine* clause in the French conveyance when you acquire French *immeubles* (afterwards it is too late). This ensures that the property passes automatically to the surviving spouse, who is free to dispose of it as he or she wishes. Unfortunately, the *tontine* does not remove the exposure to French inheritance tax and when one of the co-owner dies, the tax is charged as if a half share of the property passes to the survivor. There is only one transferee, and therefore only one exemption to set against the value of the estate.

Another point to bear in mind is that if the parties of an *acquisition en tontine* subsequently fall out, the position can be extremely messy, and it may not be easy for one of the parties to extricate himself or herself from the investment.

Couples marrying in France enter into a contract regulating their property rights. 90% of them enter into a 'community property' marriage contract, under which part or all of their property is considered to be property of the marriage (whoever may be the registered owner). The French consider that a normal British marriage gives rise to a 'separate estates' marital regime, so that property registered in the name of one spouse belongs to that spouse. It is entirely possible, however, for a couple who have been married under foreign law for many years to form a French marriage contract in relation to their French property. This device can protect the surviving spouse, and saves French inheritance tax (see below 2.6.2).

2.6.2 *French succession law and inheritance tax*

French succession law prevents individuals from disposing of their French property exactly as they would wish. When you die, certain close relatives known as *héritiers réservataires* or entrenched heirs become entitled to a *réserve légale* or reserved share in the title to your French property as of right from the moment of your death. It is important to note that French property belonging to a deceased individual will **not** pass to his surviving spouse or partner under the entrenched heirship rules. This is partly explained by the fact that, normally, much of the property belonging to the spouses is 'community property' which may pass to the surviving spouse in any event (see 2.6.1 above).

In respect of the property which belonged to the deceased, if the deceased leaves one living child (or a deceased child with living issue), that child (or the grandchildren) is entitled to a share in one-half of the French property (as a minimum). If the deceased leaves two children or their issue, their reserved share is two-thirds. If there are three or more children or their issue, they share at least three-quarters. If the deceased leaves no children or other descendants but leaves surviving ascendants in both maternal and paternal lines, their reserved share is one-half of the French property. If the deceased leaves ascendants in one line only, they share in at least one-quarter of the property.

Provided that you make a valid Will, the *quotité disponible* or remainder of your French property can pass to your surviving spouse or any other beneficiary of your choosing. If you do not make a Will, the remainder of your French property may pass under French intestacy rules to more distant family relatives (e.g. brothers and sisters) and your surviving spouse will usually only have limited rights of ownership in your share of the property.

If you have already made a Will (English or French), it will be invalid to the extent that it gives to anyone else part of your estate which, under the rules of French succession law, must go to your *réservataires*. Although a French Will is not strictly necessary if your English Will complies with these rules, the administration of your French estate under an English Will can give rise to complex and costly formalities. For example, the Will must be translated into French and certified by a French court official, notarised, and its authority proven by lengthy French language affidavits of law.

To simplify the process, and reduce the cost of winding up your estate in France, it is usually preferable to execute an English Will which excludes all reference to your French property; and a French Will limited to your French property. If you decide not to make a French Will, the solicitor chosen to draw up your English Will should be aware of the French succession law and international taxation issues which will arise when you die.

A French Will can either be *authentique, olographe* or *secret* (this last form is rarely used). The main advantage of an *authentique* Will, which must be prepared by, executed and witnessed before one or two French *notaires,* is that the date on which it was made and the capacity of the person making it cannot be questioned. It can validly be made by a testator who cannot write because he is, for example, blind or infirm. By contrast, an *olographe* Will (which must be entirely in the handwriting of and signed and dated by the testator, and does not need to be witnessed) is much simpler and cheaper to prepare. It can be executed in England and no-one needs to know of its contents. Its main disadvantages are that the testator may not know how exactly to explain his wishes (so that it is open to various interpretations); and that it can easily be destroyed if left at home. These problems can be avoided by having its contents prepared in unambiguous terms by a lawyer, and depositing the executed original with a *notaire* who will register it at the Central Wills Registry in France.

Many *notaires* advise their English clients to execute a *donation entre époux* as a method of side-stepping and solving all the succession problems which French law can impose on them. However, it does not, and the formal documentation and expenses involved achieves nothing which is not achieved by making a French Will.

Most English and French Wills contain the clause "I revoke all former Wills". A recent case saw a lady lose the French property she would otherwise have inherited under her late husband's French Will because his English solicitor had drawn up a more recent English Will, unwittingly cancelling the original French Will. To avoid these and other possible problems which can lead to costly disputes, it is important that your two Wills are drafted in such a way that one does not revoke the other.

The French tax rules encourage people to leave French property to children, parents or spouses by allowing generous nil rate bands and lower rates of gift tax.

Couples married under a community property marriage regime will benefit from a 1% registration duty in lieu of normal inheritance tax rates if the community property passes to the surviving spouse.

Transfers of assets which are not part of a marriage community property, and between husband and wife are taxable in France, after a tax-free allowance of €76,000. The rates applicable to the remainder are as follows:

Band of Value	Rate of Tax %
Less than €7,600	5
€ 7,600 to € 15,000	10
€ 15,000 to € 30,000	15
€ 30,000 to € 520,000	20
€ 520,000 to € 850,000	30
€ 850,000 to €1,700,000	35
€1,700,000 upwards	40

Transfers between ascendants and descendants or vice versa are taxed at the rates below after an abatement of €46,000 per beneficiary:

Band of Value	Rate of Tax %
Less than €7,600	5
€ 7,600 to € 11,400	10
€ 11,400 to € 15,000	15
€ 15,000 to € 520,000	20
€ 520,000 to € 850,000	30
€ 850,000 to €1,700,000	35
€1,700,000 upwards	40

Transfers between siblings are taxed as shown below, after an abatement of €1,500 per beneficiary. An unmarried brother or sister of the deceased, who is over 50 or invalid and who has lived with the deceased for the five years preceding the death, is entitled to an increased tax-free abatement of €15,000.

Band of Value	Rate of Tax %
Less than €23,000	35
€23,000 upwards	40

Transfers to cousins and second cousins are taxed at 55% after an abatement of €1,500.

Transfers to individuals not related by blood or marriage are taxed at 60% after an abatement of €1,500. The same rate applies to gifts to foreign charities, even though such gifts might have been exempt from tax in the country where the charity is based.

From 16 November 1999, unmarried couples may benefit from lower rates under the PACS or *Pacte Civil de Solidarité* arrangement. This is a contract concluded by two adults living together as a couple. The PACS is opened to both heterosexual and homosexual couples. The partners must not be closely related to each other, and neither of them may be already married or a partner in another PACS. If either partner becomes married to someone else, the PACS is dissolved. In terms of inheritance tax the partners in a PACS are entitled to an abatement of €57,000 and the rates applicable to any gifts in excess of this abatement apply as follows:

Band of Value	Rate of Tax %
Less than €15,000	40
€15,000 upwards	50

A couple in a PACS cannot enter into a community property contract so they cannot avail themselves of the most tax-efficient method of passing property from one spouse to another.

2.6.3 Ownership of French property via a company

Under Article 529 of the French Civil Code, a shareholder's interests in a company are classed as movable property and pass in accordance with the law of the country where he is habitually resident. A shareholder who remains domiciled or habitually resident in the UK can therefore dispose of his shares in a company during his lifetime or on death in accordance with English law, thereby postponing the rules of French succession law which would otherwise apply if the property were held directly by individuals en indivision or en tontine.

a) Offshore companies

Non-French resident individuals considering an investment in French property often ask whether they should form an 'offshore' (i.e. tax haven) company to own their new investment. The answer is usually in the negative for the following reasons:

● Transfers of property to tax-haven companies pay the full rate of stamp duty (currently nearly 20%).

● The French will assess the offshore company to a 3% tax per annum on the market value of the property it owns in France.

● In addition, the company will pay French corporation tax on any rental income it obtains from the property. The rate of corporation tax will normally be 33.33%, whereas an individual in receipt of rental income from France would be likely to suffer tax at the minimum rate for non-French residents which is currently 25%. The minimum corporation tax charge for companies with a turnover of between €76,000 and €150,000 is €750. The property in France could be regarded as a permanent establishment of the foreign company, in which case it may have to register its presence in France and comply with various administrative filing requirements.

● An individual is entitled to indexation relief and to write off 5% of the gain for each year of ownership beyond the second. A company is entitled to neither of these reliefs.

- The shareholders who have the use of the French property would have a personal French income tax liability calculated either as a notional income of three times the rental value of the property if they reside in countries which do not have double tax treaties with France. If they live in treaty partner countries, their own country may seek to tax them on a benefit in kind (afforded to them in the form of the rent-free occupation of the property) basis.

- Commercial companies owning French property without letting it have been known to be taxed on a notional rental income under the *acte anormal de gestion* principle (ie abnormal management).

It is conceivable that in the case of a very valuable investment, the exposure of the non-resident to French gifts, inheritance and wealth tax could call for more sophisticated planning. In this situation, however, it will generally be much simpler to reduce the size of the French estate exposed to French capital taxes by borrowing to finance the acquisition of the property.

b) Ownership of French property via an SCI

Ready-made 'off the shelf' companies do not exist in France. Companies are generally divided into those which have 'civil' objects and those which have 'commercial' objects. The test of commerciality is essentially the intention to buy and sell goods.

A *Notaire* will usually charge between €1,600 and €4,600 to incorporate and register a *Société Civile Immobilière* or civil property-holding company (the 'SCI'). Notwithstanding the costs of incorporating an SCI, there are many situations where it is desirable to use one, for example where more than one investor is involved, or where foreign investors wish to avoid the consequences of French succession law by holding only personal property in their own names.

For tax purposes, an SCI is deemed to have no existence distinct from its members and each shareholder is treated as an owner of the land. Income from unfurnished lettings is assessed on the individual shareholders and gains realised on a sale of the shares by an individual are subject to the private capital gains tax rules. A fiscally transparent company therefore allows advantage to be taken of the favourable tax treatment accorded to individuals, while using a corporate form. An SCI which lets its property out on a furnished basis is a special case, as described at 7.4. The use of an SCI is not however a universal panacea, and you should consider the burden of complying with company law and tax reporting requirements when exploring this option. It may also be difficult to raise loan finance from a French bank if a company is used.

c) Other companies

For convenience many investors choose to use a company registered in their own home country. They understand the relevant company law and can carry on the administration themselves. Provided the country of their residence has a double tax treaty with France, and they comply with the French reporting requirements, such a company will not suffer the 3% annual tax on the market value of the French property. However, it is seldom possible to make a foreign company fiscally transparent in France. The company will therefore be subject to French corporation tax and the other disadvantages applicable to offshore companies.

2.6.4 *Ownership via trusts*

The concept of the trust does not exist in French law, and if property in France is owned by a trustee, the trustee will be treated (and taxed) as the full beneficial owner. It is therefore generally not wise for a trustee to acquire French real estate.

ιAKING THE PROPERTY LETTABLE

The market for holiday lets in France is competitive and regular or return bookings are only likely if the property is well equipped and in a good structural condition.

1   RENOVATION AND CONVERSION

No 'development' (i.e. construction of a new house, a change to the outside aspect of an existing building such as replacement windows and doors, a new roof or an extension, or a change of use such as the conversion of a barn into residential quarters) should be undertaken on any property unless a *Certificat d'Urbanisme* ('CU') has been issued by the *Mairie* of the *commune* in which the property is situated confirming that your project can go ahead.

Generally speaking, planning permission (*permis de construire*) must also be obtained before any development or modernisation. Planning permission is not usually necessary for:

- fences no higher than 2 metres above ground;

- terraces no higher than 0.6 metres above ground;

- posts, aerials, etc no higher than 12 metres above ground;

- any work of less than 2 square metres in area and 1.5 metres above ground;

- statues or monuments no higher than 12 metres above ground or of no greater volume than 40 cubic metres.

Works carried out inside the property (such as bathroom or kitchen conversions) can, with certain exceptions, usually be carried out without planning permission provided they conform to local building regulations. Demolition work is often subject to planning permission, but work such as the maintenance of façades or the construction of an outdoor swimming pool can usually be undertaken without planning permission by obtaining an exemption certificate one month before the work is due to start. Depending on the region, the installation of septic tanks may also require planning permission.

French builders (*artisans*) are required to register with the local chamber of trade (*Chambre des Métiers*) and with the national standards institute (*OPQCB*) which issues certificates of competence. *Artisans* and other properly registered builders in France are required to carry insurance cover which underwrites the guarantees of the quality of their work and of its conformity with the codes of practice and building regulations.

To encourage the general upgrading of French properties, the VAT payable on renovation material and renovation work invoiced from 15 September 1999, has been reduced from 20.6% to 5.5% for a trial period of three years.

3.2   FURNITURE

Unless the property is in an area where the demand for high class-accommodation is great, furniture need not be luxurious but should be solid, comfortable and easy to maintain or clean.

Many tenants prefer separate bedrooms for the different members of their group. Double beds reduce the number of family permutations, and therefore the potential market, particularly when two or more families want to share the use of the property at the same time. Children will usually double up but relying on a sofa/folding bed for adults will not endear a property to the majority of tenants. The beds should have washable calico covers, and each bedroom should have a wardrobe. Recurrent complaints include the poor quality of beds and lack of easy chairs.

3.3   LINEN

Some landlords choose to provide linen, but it may be more trouble than it is worth, and it is not unreasonable to expect tenants to bring their own. If linen is provided tenants should be told in advance of any extra charge for cleaning sheets, towels and pillow cases at the local *blanchisserie*. It is also wise to keep a spare set of linen in case of any unexpected need. Duvets may be preferred to blankets, but this is a matter of personal choice. There should be two pillows for each bed.

3.4   KITCHEN EQUIPMENT

Poor cooking facilities are another source of complaint. There should be sufficient matching sets of crockery, cutlery, cooking utensils and other essential items which should be both durable and of reasonable quality. Tenants will not usually put up with cracked cups, burnt saucepans etc, and will expect everything provided in the kitchen and bathroom to be clean and functional.

3.5   DOMESTIC EQUIPMENT

The domestic equipment provided for the tenant's use should be in good working order and you should take out service contracts for washing machines, dish-washing machines, cooking and other appliances. Although heating is not particularly important during the summer months, some provision should be made in case of the odd cold evening, which is not unusual even during the warmest months. Efficient portable electric heaters may be the most appropriate method. If the property has central heating, the system should be turned off before each letting. The tenant can, of course, turn it on if he chooses. Whatever type of heating is provided, the power consumed should be metered and charged for. It is advisable to ensure that the central heating system is serviced regularly.

3.6 CLEANING, MAINTENANCE, CARETAKING AND RECEIVING GUESTS

A friendly neighbour or other dependable local catetaker should be retained to inspect the interior and generally keep an eye on the property throughout the year so that any problems (e.g. burst water pipes) can immediately be rectified. It is important that the property is refurbished before the start of the letting season and some annual maintenance and decoration is usually necessary.

The property should also be thoroughly cleaned before the start of each letting period.

A cold fridge stocked with basic groceries (e.g. eggs, butter and milk), hot water and a few flowers make tenants feel even more welcome.

3.7 INSURANCE AND SAFETY

It is an offence not to have minimum third party public liability insurance or *assurance à responsabilité civile* on completion of your purchase. Fire insurance cover is also obligatory. Your insurance cover should as a minimum be extended to include damage or injury to neighbours and third parties such as tenants or their guests (*recours des voisins et des tiers*). *Assurance multi-risques habitation* or householder's comprehensive insurance is an extension to the above cover which protects you not only against damage or injury to third parties but also usually covers:

- explosions, lightning and terrorist attacks;

- storms, hail and the weight of snow on roofs;

- natural disasters;

- damage to installations due to flooding or freezing;

- legal expenses;

- breakages;

- household accidents and damage to electrical appliances;

- theft and acts of vandalism.

Your insurance company should be notified that the property is being used for holiday lettings. You should also ensure that the policy is extended to cover damage caused to the property by the tenant or his guests, particularly fire and water damage. There should be no dangerous edges, traps or other hazards either inside or outside the property. Young children in particular should be considered when checking for hazards. If the property is near a road, there should be a fence or gate to prevent young children or animals running out. It is recommended that a first aid kit is provided, and put in an accessible place in the kitchen. The tenant should take out his own insurance to cover personal injury and theft or damage to his property.

The French authorities may refuse you permission to let on a commercial basis (see 6. below) if the property or its installations and equipment fail to comply with various standards, fire regulations and other safety laws. For example, all electrical wiring should be in good order and conform to the appropriate regulations and approved standards. If in doubt, a French electrical contractor should check this for you. Often, detailed plans are required, showing rooms with exit point fire doors, and an application fee will be payable. Your insurance company should be told that part of your property is to be let so that any necessary adjustments to the policy can be made.

4.   MARKETING AND MANAGEMENT

The success or failure of your letting will very much depend on how well you market your property and manage the lettings. There is an enormous choice in where to advertise, so you should aim at the widest possible audience all year round. The Internet is a must because of the number of people who now have access. Various French laws penalise landlords who advertise in a misleading way (*publicité mensongère*) or misdescribe the true quality, quantity or fitness of the property and its equipment. There are criminal fines ranging from €375 to €750 for breaches of these laws and/or imprisonment for up to four years. An injured party may sue for damages if any have been suffered and French consumer organisations may also claim damages for *préjudice public* from the landlord.

4.1   BROCHURES

You should prepare a concise and informative brochure which should contain:

- An attractive description of the area, immediate location (with a map referring to places of interest) and a photograph or drawing of the property, highlighting attractive features such as its architecture, outlook, garden and garden furniture. Invest in decent literature and make sure that photographs are without shadows, leafless trees, grey skies, or clutter in the foreground. A sunny balcony or a secluded terrace could give you the edge over other properties;

- A description of the facilities and equipment (e.g. washing machine, telephone, swimming pool) and information detailing distances to the nearest shops, restaurants, post office and sporting facilities such as golf, fishing etc;

- Details of booking periods (e.g. Saturday to Saturday), and the arrangements for receiving visitors on their arrival and handing over the keys. One major concern people have when booking properties direct with owners is that they are afraid they will have no comeback if they have cause for complaint.

- Details of the rent you charge which should to some extent be dictated by what other people charge locally, but care should be taken to compare like with like. You should also take into account the value of the French Franc against Sterling and other foreign currencies in so far as possible.

4.2   WHERE TO ADVERTISE

Advertising can be expensive and is often a matter of trial and error. Among different ways of advertising the property you may consider the following:

- National newspapers. Although effective at filling high season availability, linage adverts in the classified sections of newspapers can be very expensive if you want more than a few weeks of letting.

- Local or regional newspapers. For one small property only, it may well be more cost-effective using regional newspapers in a selected area.

- Periodical magazines are well used by self-catering property owners. Some of these magazines, such as The Lady, have pages of advertisements for holiday lettings during the height of the booking period in February and March. The cost of advertising varies considerably. There is a very wide range of choice, but some of the more unusual publications often produce the best results with the least expense. Depending on your area, an advertisement aimed at a more specialised readership might yield a good response.

- The French Government Tourist Board's nationwide and regional publications are worth considering. They are well used and, depending upon your area, are often well produced and a cost-effective place to advertise. Other publications, such as *Gîtes de France* or Brittany Ferries Magazine specialise in certain types of property, such as farm cottages. The response rate to advertisements in these annuals varies enormously. Owners of several units, or expensive property, may do well to consider these annual publications, but please note that most publishers require full details sometimes as early as June for release in the following year.

- Foreign advertising is risky for the inexperienced. Some town councils in France produce an accommodation register. It is often worthwhile to have your property listed, provided the cost is not prohibitive. Outside the U.K., the Belgians, the Dutch and the Germans are most interested in self-catering holidays in France. Agencies in the U.S. are particularly keen to take French properties onto their books. To attract overseas visitors it is often found best to locate a local agent through the tourist board in the country in question. The English Tourist Board (ETB) in London can supply the address of the tourist authority in other countries. The ETB offices in Europe are particularly helpful. If advertising is placed overseas, it should ask that replies be sent to the local agent.

4.3   LETTING AND MANAGING AGENTS

It may be more convenient to engage a letting agency to market and manage your property. French agents must have your written authority (*mandat de gestion*) to let the property and will usually ask you to sign their own short standard-form. It is important that you have this document thoroughly vetted before signature to ensure that your rights and obligations and the duties of the letting agent are clearly defined. For example, some French letting agents retain deposit cheques or rent paid by tenants and do not pay them into their bank account until the end of the tenancy or return them if they are not needed. For various legal reasons, it is important that the *mandat* states that the letting agent will immediately bank any monies received by a tenant as soon as they are received.

A number of UK-based agencies specialise in letting French property, some of which offer a complete marketing and fully-insured management service. Others do not provide local service in France and on-site cleaning, maintenance etc is therefore your responsibility.

Most agents charge commission based on a percentage of the rent charged. The percentage may vary depending on the amount of administration they are asked to carry out on your behalf. If you instruct a French letting agent on a full management basis (to include finding tenants, collecting rent, attending to any complaints, paying accounts, dealing with repairs and carrying out inspections) he will usually charge 20% of the rental plus French VAT (currently 19.6%). The fees charged by a letting or managing agent are however deductible against rental income for tax purposes.

5. LETTING AGREEMENTS

With few exceptions (see Appendix A), the rights and obligations of landlords (*bailleurs*) and of their tenants (*locataires* or *preneurs*) will be governed by French law. It is important that a written tailor-made letting agreement (*contrat de location*) containing all the appropriate clauses for your protection is prepared and signed by the parties before the tenant takes occupation of the property in France.

Many landlords agree to let their property in France to tenants on an informal verbal basis. The tenancy will then be governed by the French Civil Code which offers landlords limited protection in the event of a dispute with the tenant. Similar problems may arise if a tenancy is agreed by exchange of correspondence, or under a loosely-worded written agreement. In some cases, the landlord may be unable to repossess the property at the end of the letting period. French letting agents (*agents locataires*) often invite landlords to sign a standard-form letting agreement which may contain clauses to the landlord's disadvantage. Some of these contracts bear English translations, but many are misleading and unintelligible.

5.1 SHORT-TERM LETS OF FURNISHED PROPERTY

Most UK or other tenants will only want to rent your property for a short holiday. Under French law, a tenant or his family cannot remain in the property at the end of the letting period if, in accordance with Articles 1714 to 1762 of the French Civil Code, and other *arrêtés* or *décrets* (laws):

● They have a permanent home elsewhere. Always check the position before you allow a tenant to take occupation of your property.

● The property is adequately furnished and equipped. If you let unfurnished or inadequately furnished property (e.g. a flat which has no kitchen, table, wardrobe and/or no bed), your tenants may be able to remain there indefinitely. Cases which have gone to court in France seem to suggest that a property is adequately furnished if, as a minimum, it has a bed, table, chairs, wardrobe, refrigerator and kitchen equipment. A properly drafted letting agreement should therefore contain an inventory (*inventaire*) signed by the parties which details the furniture and equipment in the property.

● The letting period is temporary and does not overrun the 'official' holiday season (*la saison*) which varies from region to region. For example, you can let property on the Mediterranean coast in the summer months and also around Christmas time. Elsewhere, the French holiday season usually runs from June till early September, although the ski resorts have a winter and a summer season. Wherever the property is located, the tenant may be able to remain in indefinite occupation if the letting period exceeds three months (Article 1 of a law (*arrêté*) dated 8 January 1993).

- The property is only let for holiday purposes. The tenant should at no times be allowed to conduct any business or study in the property.

- The property should comply with the minimum requirements of *décret* 87-149 of 6 March 1987 which states, inter alia, that the property should be 'free of permanent noxious odours' and is 'situated away from areas likely to be a nuisance to holidaymakers' (e.g.major roads, railways and airports).

5.1.1 The landlord's main obligations

Whatever a letting agreement says, the French Civil Code states that a landlord must:

- Allow the tenant to enjoy quiet possession (*jouissance paisible*) of the property. The landlord is not, however, liable for acts of third parties which affect the tenant's rights of quiet possession (e.g. theft). The landlord may enter the property to carry out urgent structural alterations or repairs which cannot be put off until the end of the letting period;

- Ensure that the property and its equipment are in a good state of repair and fit for their intended use before the tenant takes possession, unless the tenant unreservedly accepts any imperfections which are brought to his attention before he takes occupation.

- Carry out all works necessary to keep the property and its equipment in a good state of repair whilst the tenant is in occupation.

5.1.2 The tenant's main obligations

Under the French Civil Code, a tenant must:

- Pay the agreed rent and charges in the manner prescribed by the landlord;

- Not use the property for any purposes other than those agreed;

- Not be a nuisance to neighbours and the general public during the letting period;

- Take care of the property and be responsible for any damage caused by his family and guests. If the property and/or its furniture and equipment are damaged or destroyed by fire, Article 1733 of the French Civil Code presumes the tenant to be responsible, whether or not caused deliberately or accidentally, unless the tenant can prove that the fire was caused by a structural defect, a third party, or by *force majeure*;

- Return the property to the landlord at the end of the letting period in the same state and condition as it was when he took possession.

If the tenant fails to comply with these obligations, the landlord can usually terminate the letting agreement with immediate effect and the tenant may be liable to pay the landlord rent for as long as it takes to make the property lettable again. This should be pointed out to the tenant before he takes occupation of the property.

5.2 CONTENTS OF A SHORT-TERM LETTING AGREEMENT

To protect the landlord against most foreseeable problems, a written letting agreement (see Appendix A) containing the following essential clauses should be signed and exchanged by the parties:

a) Full details of the landlord and tenants (name, address and telephone number).

b) A precise legal identification of the property (*description des lieux* or *état descriptif*) and those fixtures and fittings of which the tenant will have exclusive use (or use in common with others) during the letting period. Under a French law of 16 May 1967, a full description of the property should be supplied to and approved by the tenant before he takes up occupation. This description should detail which rooms are to be used as bedrooms; the kitchen and bathroom facilities available; parking facilities (if any) and distances to nearby facilities, e.g. the beach, ski slope, shops etc. The agreement should also state whether cutlery, linen, a telephone and/or television are provided, and whether they will be charged for separately.

c) The date and time when the letting period commences and ends, and to whom the tenant should return the keys. The tenancy will automatically be renewed if the tenant is expressly or tacitly allowed to remain in possession of the property at the end of the original letting period.

d) The amount of the rent (*loyer*). There are no legal limits on the amount of rent which can be charged for a short-term tenancy. As debt recovery procedures can be lengthy and expensive to pursue, the rent should preferably be paid in full before the tenant takes occupation of the property.

e) The amount of the deposit (*dépôt de garantie*) payable by the tenant which a prudent landlord should insist on receiving to cover the cost of repairing or replacing any damage or loss caused by the tenant or his guests to the property, its equipment or contents. An inventory of the contents should also be prepared, signed by the parties and annexed to the letting agreement before the tenant takes occupation and when he leaves. If the property and its contents are intact when the tenant leaves the property, he will recover his deposit in full. If (apart from fair wear and tear) any property damage has been done, or items listed in the inventory are broken, missing or have not been replaced, the letting agreement should state that the landlord can deduct the necessary repair or replacement costs from the deposit.

There are two types of deposit. One is called *arrhes* and the other *acompte*. If the tenant is in breach of contract, he loses his *arrhes*. He may be sued for damages as well. But if the landlord breaks the contract, he must under Article 1590 of the French Civil Code repay twice the *arrhes* to the tenant. However, if the deposit is called an *acompte* or *dépôt de garantie* and the tenant is in breach of contract, again it is lost and he risks a claim for damages. But the landlord in breach only has to pay back what he received – and is not under the immediate penalty of double repayment. He may well be faced with a legal action for breach of contract, but that costs money and takes time. It is therefore essential that **any** prepayment should be described on a receipt, invoice or letting agreement as a *dépôt de garantie* or an *acompte*.

f) A schedule of condition (*état des lieux*) can also be agreed and signed by the parties before the tenant takes occupation. This can be prepared by a letting agent in France. In the absence of a schedule of condition, the French Civil Code provides that the tenant is presumed to have taken the property in a good state of repair, unless there is evidence to the contrary.

g) The amount of any extra charges for the use or consumption of water, electricity, gas and telephone. Many landlords charge a fixed amount (*charge forfaitaire*) for the supply of services. In some areas, a local *taxe de séjour* (tourist tax) may also apply.

h) A list of 'house rules' to avoid possible arguments or complaints about, for example, loud music, unwelcome pets or anything else which might prove disruptive to neighbours or the general public. The letting agreement should also allow the landlord or his agents to inspect the property at regular intervals to keep an eye on the tenants or carry out any urgent structural alterations or repairs, no matter what nuisance this causes the tenants or whether they are deprived of the use of all or part of the property. It is possible to insert a 'penalty clause' in the agreement, whereby a defaulting tenant is liable to pay a fixed sum penalty (which can be deducted from the deposit) if he fails to respect the house rules.

i) If there are two or more tenants, the name of one tenant who will be personally liable for the rent, deposit and other charges, thereby enabling the landlord to sue that tenant for any losses if the other tenants refuse to pay or are in breach of the 'house rules'.

j) A clause dealing with the assignment or sub-letting of the property. The letting agreement should provide that the landlord can immediately repossess the property and keep the deposit in full if the tenants allow friends or others who are not named in the letting agreement to take occupation of the property. It is an offence under French law to use or threaten force and harassment to gain entry into property, even when the occupants are there without the landlord's consent. A tenant who has been evicted in this way can also sue the landlord for damages and obtain a court order allowing him return to the property and remain in occupation for as long as he wishes.

k) A provision that the landlord is not responsible for loss or damage to the tenant's personal property.

5.3 LETTING FURNISHED PROPERTY FOR MORE THAN SIX MONTHS

Agreements to let furnished property in France for more than 6 months duration must be in writing and in the French language. A model form of letting agreement appears in Appendix A.3 which illustrates the terms and conditions which should be included. A prudent landlord should always have a letting agreement tailored to his requirements and approved by suitably qualified lawyers.

5.4 LETTING UNFURNISHED PROPERTY IN FRANCE

There is a large demand for long-term lets of unfurnished property in France which are governed by the Law of 6 July 1989 as amended by a Law of 21 July 1994. Although this type of letting is beyond the scope of this book, British landlords should be warned that their obligations are more onerous than if they let property on a furnished basis. The minimum letting period is usually three years if the landlord is a private individual (six years if a company). The landlord must give the tenant at least six months notice to quit the property and the grounds enabling him to repossess the property during the letting period are limited.

5.5 LETTING LAND

Do not allow farmers or anyone else the *usage agricole* (use for agricultural purposes such as pasture or cultivation) of your land in France in return for rent – no matter how small the payment – or other 'consideration' (e.g. a gift, or any produce he has farmed on your land) until you have checked your legal position carefully.

The farmer ('tenant') and his successors may otherwise be protected by strict French laws which, inter alia, entitle him to an agricultural tenancy (*bail rural*) over your land. If you ('landlord') wish to sell your property, the tenant has first rights to buy the freehold. If he does not want to buy, you can sell to a third party but the tenancy will continue, which may deter a potential buyer from proceeding.

French agricultural tenancies are often very informal and, although usually made in writing, can be created verbally. It is important that a formal tailor-made agreement containing all the clauses for your protection is prepared and signed by the parties **before** the tenant begins to use your land.

Whatever the terms of your agreement, French law states that the tenancy runs for a period of at least 9 years on payment of a specified (usually low) rent. The tenant can transfer the tenancy to his spouse or adult descendants. He or his successors can renew the tenancy for a further 9 years and so on every nine years. Unless the tenant agrees to terminate the agreement, the landlord can only repossess his land if the tenant fails to pay two rental payments; or engages in bad-husbandry (i.e. activities which adversely affect the proper running of the land); or fails to carry out any improvement recommended by the local *Commission Consultative*.

The landlord should declare any rental income received for French income tax purposes (see chapter 7). Where the income exceeds €1,830 during the tax year (calendar year) on a property over 15 years old, the landlord may also suffer a tax on leases called *contribution sur les revenus locatifs* (see section 7.3.3).

If you receive no payment or other 'consideration', none of the above legal or tax provisions applies. Similarly, no agricultural tenancy exists if you employ a gardener (or other non-farmer) to maintail land close to your buildings. Other exceptions include tenancies of woods, forests, small areas of land (depending on the *département*, usually limited to one or two hectares).

If you employ a gardener or other full/part time employee in France, the contract of employment must comply with the *Code du Travail* which limits the length of the working week and provides, inter alia, for a minimum wage, holiday entitlement and paid maternity leave. The procedure for dismissing an employee in France is very formalistic. You must also register with URSSAF, ASSEDIC and other bodies and pay French Social Security contributions which will represent about 40% of the employee's gross salary.

A friendly neighbour or other dependable local caretaker in France should be able to maintain the upkeep of your garden and land on an informal basis. If you feel that this can only be achieved by engaging the services of a local farmer, but do not want to grant an agricultural tenancy, a written *convention d'occupation précaire* (bare licence agreement) should be prepared by a qualified French lawyer. A properly drawn *convention* will avoid all of the potential legal and tax problems mentioned above.

6. LETTING AS A BUSINESS

There is good potential for profits if you buy:

- several residential properties;

- a large residential property for use by several different tenants at the same time;

- a *gîte*, bed and breakfast, *café*, bar, restaurant, hotel or other business (in some cases, a swimming pool, tennis court, bar, restaurant and other 'para-hotel' facilities such as a daily maid are also provided);

- a commercial property for occupation by tenants who intend to run their own business.

The procedure for buying or selling a commercial property in France is similar to that for residential property. However, to ensure that you set the business venture off on the right foot, you should be aware of the following points:

6.1 FRENCH TRANSFER DUTY

Under the French Commercial Code, a landlord is classified as a tradesman ('*commerçant*') and must register with the local *Chambre de Commerce* within two months of commencing trading if:

- the property is owned in the name of a commercial company (see 6.2.3 below); or

- the property is classed as commercial rather than residential or is residential in character but is run as a business. This will be the case if, for example, the property comprises or is intended to comprise more than 5 furnished self-contained rooms or units for let on a systematic basis. The meaning of the word 'systematic' does not necessarily mean that the unit or room must be let on a regular basis, but that it is available for let throughout the holiday season or for longer periods. Rooms and units which share the use of a kitchen, bathroom or other facilities and equipment may still be treated as being 'self-contained' for these purposes.

With effect from 1 January 1999, transfers of properties, which fall into one of the above categories, attract a transfer registration duty of 4.8% instead of the 18.2% rate applicable before then.

6.2 STRUCTURING THE INVESTMENT

Although in general terms it is simpler and cheaper to run a business in France as an individual or group of individuals, the transfer duty problem can be avoided by owning a commercial property (*les murs*) in France through the medium of a

French civil company (the 'SCI') provided that the SCI does not itself engage in commercial activities but delegates this task to a separate company.

This type of structure can not only help to secure the maximum tax advantage whilst retaining the benefit of limited liability against the commercial risks inherent in the business, but also circumvent the effects of French succession law. It is possible to use a UK or other non-French company structure but for tax reasons this option is rarely beneficial.

6.2.1 *The property*

Although you can either buy a residential or a commercial property (freehold or leasehold), it may be easier to buy an existing business in France than to create a new one. If you want to buy the freehold of the property and (if there is one) the existing business at the same time, there will usually be two separate contracts. If you do not have a large amount to invest, you may be able to purchase the *fonds de commerce* only and take a lease (*bail*) of the property from the landlord with an option to purchase the freehold from him at a later date.

Leases of business or commercial premises in France are governed by Law 53.960 of 30 September 1953. As a general rule, a business lease may not be for less than nine years. A business tenant generally has security of tenure and is entitled to compensation if his lease is not renewed in cases where the law so allows.

6.2.2 *The business*

If you buy an existing *fonds de commerce* the registration tax payable is a fixed charge of €15 up to €23,000 and a rate of 4.8% of the value exceeding €23,000.

The *fonds de commerce* will often be owned and managed by a French limited liability 'commercial' company which pays rent to the SCI or other entity which owns the freehold or leasehold of the property. In many cases, the shareholders in the SCI and the commercial company will be owned by the same individuals. In addition to the advantages of setting up or buying into this type of structure, if the business does not work out, your property will remain in the ownership of the SCI, which will not necessarily be affected by the failure of the company which runs the business. You can sell the business, but keep the property, thereby drawing an income from the lease of the property to whoever purchases your business. The rent paid by the commercial company is deducted from its income or profits which are subject to French corporation tax. This structure is also an advantage for the new owner, as it reduces the amount of initial capital required by him to take over the business.

6.2.3 French commercial companies

There are two ways of carrying on a business in France. The first is as a sole trader (*entreprise individuelle*) and the second is through a corporate body (*société*).

Although an *entreprise individuelle* is the smallest form of business organisation and the simplest to run, it does not have the protection of limited liability. A sole trader is personally liable for all debts arising in connection with his business. By contrast, the liability of the members for the debts of a *société*, depending on its type, may or may not be limited.

In France, the first broad category of *société* corresponds to an English law partnership where the members have unlimited liability for the debts of the *société*. The second category corresponds approximately under English law to a limited liability company where the liability of members is usually limited to their investment in the capital of the company.

The two most popular forms of limited liability company structures in France are the SARL (*Société à Responsabilité Limitée*) and the SA (*Société Anonyme*). An SARL corresponds to an English private limited company. The SA is similar to an English public limited company in its structure and purpose.

One relative advantage of a SARL over an SA is that a SARL only requires two members with a total of €7,500 in capital, whereas forming a SA requires seven shareholders to contribute a total of €37,000. Moreover, an SA's balance sheet must be published publicly, but a SARL's can remain private.

One of the disadvantages of a SARL relative to the SA form is that shares in a SARL must be entirely paid-up at the time of incorporating the company. Only one-quarter of the nominal value of an SA's shares have to be paid-up when issued, the remainder can be payable over five years.

An SARL may not issue negotiable bonds. Consequently all financing must derive from bank loans and investment by members. The SA is the only limited liability company structure that can issue various types of negotiable securities and offer its shares to the public. It is therefore the appropriate form of business structure for operations whose capital requirements are large and cannot be satisfied by a restricted number of shareholders, or which need to offer negotiable shares and bonds to finance their growth.

The SA is usually considered to be more suitable to large scale operations in view of its more complicated management and control structure. The SARL is extensively used by businessmen who wish to use a limited liability vehicle without using the more complex form of an SA in the context of small to medium size operations.

Other forms of commercial company exist, in particular the société en nom collectif ('SNC') – a general partnership – and the société en commandite simple ('SCS') which is a limited partnership. The SCS has many tax and legal advantages when the management team, composed of individuals, is unable to put much equity into the company but wishes and deserves not only to have an efficient incentive by way of sharing in the profits but also to enjoy a certain independence vis a vis the shareholders (e.g. venture capitalists). The main problem of this form, ie the unlimited liability of the general partner, can easily be solved as a general partner can itself be a limited company (SA or SARL).

The SNC, which is not subject to French corporation tax, is often used within French industrial groups for subsidiaries contemplating losses which can, in this case, be deducted at parent level.

Since 1994 there has been a new form of company called a société par actions simplifiées which is a vehicle for joint ventures between very large corporations.

Whatever the form of company, the legal incorporation and publicity formalities involved take about 15 days after the execution of the by-laws and the payment of the share capital to be issued (100% for a SARL, 25% for a SA) into a special account opened with a bank where the money is kept in escrow until the delivery of the certificate of incorporation by the Registre du Commerce et des Sociétés.

By-laws and minutes of general meetings do not need to be executed in the presence of a Notaire. If the by-laws so permit, general meetings of shareholders and the meetings of the Board can be held outside France.

With the exception of dealing with the formalities relating to the remaining foreign exchange controls (which are about to be greatly reduced), French companies controlled by foreigners are treated in exactly the same way as other French companies.

6.3   RUNNING A BUSINESS IN FRANCE

As a *commerçant*, you should at least have a reasonable knowledge of spoken French in order to keep on top of the administration and comply with the various tax and other official documents you will receive each year, failing which you may face a hefty fine. The Chambre de Commerce may run a *stage de gestion* (management course) for the small business. In some cases, the course is compulsory. The local *Chambre des Métiers* may also, at reasonable cost, offer to help you deal with some or all of the paperwork involved in running the operation in France. Language barriers apart, the officers at the *Chambre de Commerce*, the tax office and other administrative authorities are usually very helpful.

6.3.1 Planning permission

Planning permission must usually be obtained before your property can be used or converted for use by members of the public. The application should be sent to the local *Mairie* who will consult with the public health, fire and other authorities before permission is granted. Permission may be refused if, for example, the property is unhygienic or does not comply with the provisions of *décret* No 73-1007 of 31 October 1973 which protects the public against risks of fire and panic.

6.3.2 Sale or supply of alcohol

The licensing of premises where alcohol and soft drinks are consumed is strictly regulated by the *Code des débits de boissons*. You cannot obtain a *licence* (licence) before completing a *déclaration préalable* (prior declaration) which must be filed with the *Mairie* (in some cases, the *Préfecture de Police*) at least 15 days before the opening date. A further declaration must also be made to the *recette locale des douanes et droits indirects* who are primarily responsible for French VAT and other indirect taxes. Applications are usually processed within a fortnight.

Proprietors of restaurants, hotels and *chambres d'hôtes* who serve drinks (even free of charge) with main meals and as accompaniments to food must hold a *licence restaurant*. A *petite licence* is required where only soft drinks, beers, wines and other alcohol with a content of less than 3% are provided. If spirits and other drinks with an alcohol content of up to 18% are also served, you must hold a *grande licence restaurant*. Hotel and restaurant licences can be obtained relatively easily with no limit on numbers.

It is harder to obtain a licence to serve alcohol and soft drinks if food is **not** served on the premises. The authorities cannot issue new licences in excess of the permitted number per *département* at any one time. Nor can you transfer an existing licence from premises in (say) Paris to Marseille. A *Licence I (boissons sans alcool)* permits the sale of soft drinks only. *Licence II (boissons fermentées)* holders can also sell wines, beers and other drinks with an alcohol content of less than 3%. A *Licence III (restreinte)* authorises the sale of the above and drinks with an alcohol content of no more than 18%. Finally, a *Licence IV (de plein exercice)* holder can sell all these drinks as well as spirits. In popular resorts, a *Licence IV* will be very expensive to buy. A proprietor who does not hold a valid *licence* or who is otherwise in breach of the *Code des débits de boissons* can face heavy fines and other civil or criminal penalties. In serious cases, premises can be closed for up to twelve months by order of the *administration*.

6.3.3 Restaurants and hotels

It is important to ensure that an alcohol licence is being sold with the business and no purchase commitment should be made until this point has been carefully checked. You may also want to prevent your vendor from opening a rival establishment within a certain radius of the property in which case this should be agreed in writing before you sign a contract.

Before you can open a restaurant or hotel in France to the public, the property must first be inspected by a number of administrative bodies and a licence obtained to ensure that the establishment complies with strict safety and hygiene standards. You must also register the business at the local *Chambre de Commerce*.

6.3.4 Employment law and social security

If you employ a cook, cleaner, gardener or other full/part time employee in France, the contract of employment must comply with the *Code du Travail* which limits the length of the working week and provides, inter alia, for a minimum wage, holiday entitlement and paid maternity leave. The procedure for dismissing an employee in France is very formalistic.

You must also register with 'URSSAF', 'ASSEDIC' and other bodies and pay Social Security contributions which will represent about 40% of the employee's gross salary.

7. TAXATION

The tax year in France is the year to 31 December. The basic tax law in France is the *Code Général des Impôts* ('CGI') which is subject to frequent amendment, both by specific *lois fiscales* and the annual *loi de finances*.

A French resident taxpayer will normally deal with one of more than 800 *Centres des impôts*, appropriate to the place where he lives. Non-residents will normally deal with the *Centre des Impôts des Non-Résidents* at 9, rue d'Uzès, 75094 Paris Cedex 02.

A UK resident who lets out a property in France will have a UK liability to income tax computed under the Schedule A rules. He will be entitled to credit against his UK tax bill for the French tax which he has paid on his French rental income.

7.1 TAXATION OF RENTAL INCOME FROM FRENCH PROPERTIES OWNED BY NON-RESIDENTS

7.1.1 Self declaration

Income from letting French property must be declared to the French authorities by 30 April in each year, even if neither the owner or the tenant of the property reside in France. The onus is on the taxpayer (and not his letting or other agent) to complete and submit the returns which the law obliges him to make. A non-resident taxpayer can also be asked to designate a tax representative in France.

Whether intentionally or unintentionally, many UK and other non-resident landlords fail to declare their rental income to the French tax authorities. This lax attitude has to some extent been encouraged by the historic nonchalance of the French tax offices, although more recently French tax inspectors have been reviewing cadastral and other property records, letting agents' records and small advertisements in local French and foreign newspapers to trace undeclared lettings.

7.1.2 Penalties for late payment or filing incorrect returns

If a non-resident does not submit a return, the administration may send him a return with a *demande de déclaration* asking him to complete and submit it. The next step is that the administration sends a reminder to him (called a *mise en demeure*). If he then fails to regularise the position within 30 days, the administration can issue an estimated assessment (*taxation d'office*). The onus is then on the taxpayer to disprove the assessment. Interest on overdue tax is charged at 0.75% per month and there is a penalty of 10% if the taxpayer has made his return late but before he receives the *mise en demeure*, or if he responded within 30 days of receiving the *mise en demeure*. The penalty increases to 40% thereafter and to 80% if the taxpayer does not respond to a second *mise en demeure*.

The tax office can assess up to 3 years in arrears, and needless to say, this can give rise to heavy tax bills.

7.2 BASIS OF ASSESSMENT

7.2.1 Residence

If you are habitually resident in France, you are entitled to tax reductions for various home ownership expenses in respect of a principal residence, but these tax reductions are not normally available to non-residents. Your taxable rental income will be added to your general income and taxed according to the 'barème de l'impôt' (income tax scale) after taking your family circumstances and charges into account.

Certain non-resident individuals who let their French property are subject to French income tax on a notional income (base forfaitaire) equal to three times the rental value of the property, unless their French rental income is greater. However this does not apply to individuals resident in the UK or residents of most of the other countries that have double tax treaties with France. The people concerned by this charge include residents of the Channel Islands, the Isle of Man, Andorra and Monaco.

An individual who is affected will have to pay the charge even if he does not let out the property or has the use of the property for only part of the year. If he lets the property, the rental value is that specified in his letting agreement or lease unless this appears artificially low. If he has more than one property in France, the charge is based on 3 times the total rental values of all the properties. The income so determined is the final taxable income, and the non-resident cannot claim to deduct any home ownership expenses or other charges (see below) against income, or any losses on rented properties. The only silver lining to this cloud is that the minimum income tax rate of 25% (see below) is not applied to non-residents assessed on this basis.

A UK or other resident individual in a French treaty partner country who owns residential property in France is protected from the notional income basis of assessment and will not normally have a liability to French income tax unless he lets the property out. He will be taxed at a minimum rate of 25% on his French rental income, but the taxable amount will vary depending on the elements described below. Losses can only be set against other rental income liable to income tax in France and can be carried forward for 5 years. UK residents can set French tax paid against tax levied in the UK in respect of their French rental income (see 7.6 below). However, if a UK resident owns the property through the medium of a company, it is possible that he may be assessed to tax on the benefit-in-kind of the rent-free use of the property.

7.2.2 Unfurnished property

If an unfurnished property is let commercially by an individual, either directly or through the medium of an SCI or other fiscally transparent company, the rental income is assessable under the *revenus fonciers* rules. The income is normally reported on forms 2042 and 2044 which then need to be submitted to the *Centre des Impôts des Non-Résidents* ('CINR') in Paris.

Income from unfurnished lettings is calculated on a calendar year basis, and is generally exempt from VAT. The net taxable amount is determined depending on the level of annual rents received. If the total gross annual rental income does not exceed €15,000, the landlord is automatically assessed under the *Micro-Foncier* regime. Under this regime 40% of the gross rent is deducted as representing the total amount of expenses relating to the letting. The €15,000 limit applies for the whole tax year and is adjusted pro-rata temporis if the activity only takes place during part of the year. The limit is not pro-rated for the year when the letting activity started or ended. The *Micro-Foncier* does not apply to landlords who benefit from other tax advantages, such as owners of historic monuments and landlords who benefit from accelerated depreciation allowances. Property rentals carried out through a *société civile immobilière* are excluded from the *Micro-Foncier* regime.

Landlords under the scope of the *Micro-Foncier* regime may opt for the normal *Foncier* regime described below simply by filing the necessary annex tax form 2044 when they declare their rental income. This option is irrevocable for five years. However the administration has allowed for a 'get out' clause for taxpayers, who having opted out of the *Micro-Foncier* for 2001, now have 'second thoughts'. Indeed anyone in this position is allowed to revert back to the *Micro-Foncier* in 2003 in respect of their 2002 rental income if they so wish.

Lettings outside the scope of the *Micro-Foncier* are assessed under the normal *Foncier* regime, which allows the deduction of a wide range of expenses, as and when they are paid and as follows:

● Local property tax, *taxes foncières* (tax on land and building). The tenant should normally pay the *taxe d'habitation* (occupier's rate) if he was occupying the property as at 1 January of the tax year. If the *taxe d'habitation* is paid by the landlord then the latter is entitled to recharge this cost to the tenant.

● *Contribution sur les revenus locatifs* (tax on leases, see 7.3.3)

● repairs and maintenance;

● management expenses (*concierges*, *gérants* or *administrateurs d'immeubles*);

- improvements (such as the cost of installing central heating, lifts, telephones etc);

- interest on all debts incurred in the acquisition, construction, repair or improvement of the property, and also interest on debts incurred to preserve the owner's title to the property (e.g. interest on a loan taken out to pay inheritance tax on the property). There is no limit on the amount of interest that is deductible or to the period of time during which the interest on the loan may be deducted. The costs of borrowing (e.g. bank facility fees) are equally deductible. If the interest is incurred in the course of constructing a property and before the property is let, it can be offset against rental income from other properties let by the taxpayer, or it can be carried forward as a loss against future rental income;

- premiums for insurance against unpaid rent and any expenses that should have been (but were not) paid by the tenants and were met by the landlord;

- a *forfait* deduction of (currently) 14% of gross rental income (or 25% of rental income for shareholders in a *société civile de placement immobilier*) to cover management expenses not covered above such as telephone, travel, correspondence, house insurance, accounting, legal and tax advice, and letting agents fees.

When claiming such deductions one must ensure that evidence of all expenses incurred is available for further checking. In addition, where rural property is let, it is accepted that the 14% *forfait* deduction does not cover the cost of insurance, and the actual cost may be claimed, along with the cost of improvements to barns and other installations which are not habitable.

Losses on the letting of unfurnished property may be carried forward for up to ten years.

7.2.3 Furnished property

If a property is let furnished by an individual on an habitual basis, the income is normally assessed under the rules for business income (*bénéfices industriels et commerciaux*). However, if the accommodation let is part of the principal residence of the landlord:

- the income is totally exempt if the accommodation constitutes the principal residence of the tenant; and

- if it does not constitute the principal residence of the tenant, income of up to €760 is exempt (e.g. for the letting of guest rooms and *chambres d'hôtes*).

Under the business income rules, the assessable income will be determined on a forfeit basis, a simplified real basis or the normal basis depending on the annual turnover and the tax status of the landlord. For individuals, the taxable income will be calculated on one of the following bases:

i) *Micro BIC*

If the rental receipts are currently less than €76,300, and the letting is considered as a non-professional activity, the taxpayer will normally be assessed on the *Micro BIC* regime. Only 30% of the gross rental income is subject to taxation, since 70% is deducted to cover all charges and expenses of the letting. At first glance this method seems generous, but the result is always a profit even when the activity in fact generates losses.

ii) *Régimes réels*

The *Régime réel normal* or *Régime réel simplifié* methods of taxation – under which the actual expenses are estimated or calculated – is sometimes more advantageous. If the rental receipts are above €76,300 but below €763,000 (excluding VAT), the income will be calculated under the *réel simplifié* regime. If the rental receipts are over €763,000, the income must be calculated on the *réel normal* basis.

The difference between the *réel simplifié* basis and the *réel normal* basis of calculating income lies primarily in the level of formality to be observed in the accounting. As a non-resident, the *réel* regimes involve correspondence with both the local tax office and the tax office in Paris. The election for one or other taxation method must be made to the tax office before 1 February of the year for which the new method would be applicable. In other words, an option filed on 1 February 2003 would apply to income arising during 2003. The option is irrevocable for a period of two years. Businesses subject to the *réel simplifié* regime prepare accounts (for VAT purposes and eventually for income tax purposes) on a quarterly basis.

The expenses that may be deducted when taxable income is calculated on a *réel simplifié* or *réel normal* basis are listed below.

Companies are excluded from the *Micro BIC* regime and therefore calculate their income under one of the *réel* regimes. If the property is let by a company subject to French corporation tax (see below), the basis period is the accounting year ended in the tax year and accounts are prepared on an accruals basis.

7.2.4 Deductible expenses

Where the property is treated as a business asset (see below), the expenses relevant to property income that are deductible under the *réel* regimes are:

- The general expenses of the business. These do not include expenses which are required to be capitalized, for example the costs associated with acquiring a property or architects' fees. Such payments are added to the cost of the property and may be depreciated. However, Notarial fees, registration taxes and estate agents fees are treated as expenses. The general costs of the business include interest and bank charges paid or payable, the costs of insurance and the costs of repairs and maintenance.

- Depreciation, which on residential housing is 1 to 2% of the cost of the property on a straight line basis.

- Provisions, for example, for doubtful debts and *taxes foncières* payable. Provisions for the expenses of construction or reconstruction or fitting out a property are not allowable.

However, if the property is put at the disposal of directors or shareholders for less than a market rent, the expenses relating to the period when the directors or shareholders occupy the property are not deductible.

7.2.5 Business asset

When declaring income from a furnished property, the taxpayer must decide whether the property will be treated as a business or personal asset as this will affect the tax computation.

An individual whose rental income is less than €23,000 is normally classed as a 'non-professional landlord'. This means that he cannot deduct any losses on his rental activity from his other income (the losses can be carried forward for 5 years against future rental income) and any capital gain realised on a disposal of the property is taxed under the private capital gains tax rules.

If the taxpayer is registered at the local *registre de commerce* and either the rental income constitutes more than 50% of his total income and his rental receipts exceed €23,000, he is classed as a professional landlord. This means that he can offset any losses on his rental activity against his total income and any gain resulting from the sale of the property will be taxed as a business capital gain.

It should be borne in mind that the capital gains of a fiscally transparent company engaged in letting furnished property are exempt from capital gains tax if its turnover is less than €152,600.

7.2.6 Choosing the right basis of assessment

Needless to say, one needs to compare all the options as the resulting tax bill may vary significantly. The options also need to be chosen very carefully as they can hide some pitfalls. For instance, if your annual rental income is below

€763,000, you are by law, assessable under the *Micro BIC* regime. However, you may opt for the *régime réel*, provided you apply before 1 February of the tax year for which the option is made. The option is irrevocable for a two-year period.

Where your property is registered as a business asset, and if your rental income currently exceeds €23,000, you will automatically be regarded as a professional landlord. If you should later wish your property to be treated as a personal asset, this reclassification will give rise to professional capital gains taxes as such a transfer is treated like a sale. Bearing in mind that the limit of €23,000 (annual rents received) takes into account the notional income reported for your personal use of the property, it is quite easy to overstep this limit.

There would be no capital gains tax charge on reclassification of the property from the business asset to the personal assets category where annual rental income does not exceed the €23,000 limit, as the landlord is then considered as a non-professional. Transfers at no value under this status do not therefore qualify as a sale.

7.3   OTHER FRENCH TAXES

French income tax is not the only tax applicable to French rental income. Lettings of furnished or unfurnished properties are liable, in some cases, to French VAT ('TVA'), business tax (*taxe professionnelle*) and, if the annual rental income from the letting exceeds €1,030, a tax called *contribution sur les revenus locatifs* is also payable.

7.3.1   *TVA*

The letting of furnished property is subject to TVA if the receipts of the taxpayer currently exceed €763,000 and the property is a:

● registered tourist hotel and bed and breakfast lodging;

● registered tourist residence on a nine-year lease to a business which advertises abroad;

● Quasi – hotel business which provides, in addition to accomodation, hotel - like services (meals, cleaning, reception etc);

● property let (furnished or unfurnished) under a commercial lease to a busiess engaged in one of the activities described above.

Any lettings which do not match one of these categories are exempt from TVA.

When subject to TVA, the supply of furnished premises is charged at the reduced rate of 5.5%. However, the supply of food, telephone and other services is subject to TVA at the standard rate of 19.6%.

7.3.2 Taxe professionnelle

The business tax is due on most types of rental income with the exception of:

- one off 'incidental' lettings;

- the letting of part of one's principal residence, even on a regular basis, provided the price is reasonable;

- the letting of a property classified as a *Gîte de France* or *Meublé de Tourisme*;

- any other lettings of property which are used by the owner outside the letting season.

Although the exemption is a statutory right, provided the conditions listed above are fulfilled, it can be contested by any one of the local authorities (*Commune*, *Département* or *Région*).

7.3.3 Tax on leases

This tax applies on rental income, which is not subject to VAT. It includes any income received for the letting of fishing or hunting rights as well as furnished or unfurnished lets.

Known as the *droit de bail et contribution additionnelle* up to 1999, and then *contribution représentative du droit de bail* (CRDB) *et contribution additionnelle à la contribution représentative du droit de bail* (CACRDB), the tax on leases has undergone a number of changes in recent years. In a nutshell the CRDB applies to all 2000 lettings if the 1999 annual turnover was in excess of FrF 36,000 (FrF 12,000 prior to that date). A further charge, the CACRDB, applied if the property was over 15 years old and the rental income exceeded FrF 12,000. The rate was 2.5% for both taxes and calculated on the following taxable amount:

- the total rents received during the calendar year, plus

- any expenses normally payable by the landlord but paid by the tenants, less

- expenses paid by the landlord for the tenant (gas, electricity, water, and so on).

The landlord was able to recover the CRDB from his tenants and in the case of long-term lets this was the normal practice. The CACRDB charge was always met by the landlord.

The CRDB was suppressed as from 1 January 2001. However, the CACRDB remains in existence for the letting of properties over 15 years old if the rental income exceeds €1,830. The name of the tax has been changed to *contribution sur les revenus locatifs*, but the taxable basis and the rate remain the same.

Individuals assessed on a notional income as described above (see 7.2.1) are not liable to the *contribution sur les revenus locatifs*.

7.4   FRENCH CORPORATION TAX

French corporation tax (*impôt sur les sociétés*) is not a tax on French companies. It is a tax on the income of certain types of companies carrying on business in France. It does not apply to French companies carrying on business outside France or to French companies which are not 'capital' companies (e.g. SCIs). But it does apply to foreign 'capital' companies carrying on business in France.

Foreign capital companies are subject to French corporation tax on the profits of any business carried on in France. This is a very different basis from that which applies for income tax. There are three bases on which a French or foreign capital company can be said to be carrying on a business in France:

● it has a permanent establishment in France;

● it has a dependent agent in France;

● it habitually carries out a complete commercial cycle in France (e.g. purchase and sale).

Under many French double income tax treaties, a company is exempt from French corporation tax in respect of the profits of a trade or business if it is a resident of the treaty partner country and does not trade in France through a permanent establishment.

It is important to note that a French civil company (an 'SCI' – see 2.6.3(b) and 6.2) which rents out **furnished** accommodation is subjected to French corporation tax if its receipts from this activity constitute more than 10% of its turnover. This treatment arises because the letting of **furnished** accommodation is considered to be a commercial activity. A French SCI with UK resident shareholders and directors may well be regarded as resident in the UK, both under UK domestic law and under the provisions of Article 3 of the France-UK Income Tax Treaty. In this case the company will be liable to corporation tax in the UK, with credit for the French corporation tax suffered on its income.

These concepts are complicated and expert advice should always be sought before structuring your ownership of French property and/or the letting business through the vehicle of a French or foreign company.

7.5   TAXATION OF PROPERTY SPECULATORS

Profits realised by persons who trade in land (*marchands de biens*), profits of buying land with the intention of selling it after breaking it up into lots (*lotissements*) and profits of building (*profits de construction*) are calculated according to the business income rules and subject to income tax or corporation tax depending on the taxpayer. Building profits but must be calculated according to the *réel normal* or *réel simplifié* regimes (see 7.2.3). The question of whether a taxpayer is trading is essentially one of fact. Habitual operations carried out with a speculative intention are trading. With companies, the objects of the company and the business activities of the shareholders are taken into account.

Non-residents who engage in the activities described above are subject to a withholding tax of 50% on their profits.

7.6   LIABILITY TO TAX IN THE UK

Having properly declared and paid your taxes in France, you must then declare your rental income to the UK Inland Revenue. You can claim a credit for any French tax paid and you will only be taxed again to the extent that your liability to UK income tax exceeds the rate at which you were charged in France. So, if you are a higher rate taxpayer in the UK but have only been charged the minimum rate (25%) in France, you will be required to pay the difference to the Inland Revenue. Conversely, if you were charged a higher rate in France than your UK liability you will not be able to claim a refund for the difference.

Until the 1995 Finance Act came into force, the UK Revenue were notoriously reluctant to accept that the letting of a holiday home in France qualified as a business for UK tax purposes. They therefore generally denied relief against UK tax for any interest on money borrowed to acquire the property. Section 41 of the Finance Act changes the whole basis of the taxation of rental income from overseas properties. Although this source of income will still be assessed under Schedule D Case V, virtually all lettings of property in France will constitute part of a single 'Schedule A business', so that income on one property can be relieved against losses on another. Interest relief is available on the same basis as any other business expense, so that relief is available for interest on loans taken out to repair a French property or in respect of a vacant property (provided the property was acquired for the purposes of the business).

APPENDIX A: PRECEDENTS

PREFACE

The following precedents have been included as a guide only. Expert advice should always be obtained before completing any letting agreement.

a) Language

Most of the precedents appearing below are in French. Superficially, it is interesting to see English language translations of French legal documents but there is little merit in providing these in a book of this nature. Literal translations usually make nonsense reading. On the other hand, to provide translations in wholly 'correct' English legal phraseology implies that the French law attached to the wording used in the original language is the same as attaches to the English translation. For example, it is not safe to translate the technical terms relating to repairs in a French lease by the use of phrases so commonly found in repairing covenants in English leases.

All French documents, of whatever kind, should be initialled by all the parties on each page as well as being signed on the last page. There is no need to have witnesses.

Strictly speaking, every translation from English into French for official use, i.e. by a *Notaire*, a Court or a local Companies Registry should be made by a *traducteur juré* or assermenté (sworn translator) in France, the cost of which can be very high and the end product not always wholly accurate. In certain cases, it can be well worthwhile approaching a suitable Notary Public in the UK whose translations are accurate and acceptable in France.

A Glossary will be found in Appendix C. It has been prepared for the reader who is not familiar with French legal phraseology and to avoid the need to resort to continuous translations and explanations in the text itself.

b) Jurisdiction

Under Article 16 (1) of the 1968 Brussels Convention, most disputes concerning tenancies of French property concluded for temporary private use for a maximum period of six consecutive months can be subject to the jurisdiction of the Courts of England and Wales if:

a) The landlord and the tenant are both natural persons (i.e. neither is a company);

b) The landlord and the tenant are both domiciled in England and Wales.

In every other case, the letting agreement must always be subject to the jurisdiction of the French courts and must be written in the French language (see A.2 below).

If (English) tenants refuse to leave the property at the end of the letting period, the matter must always be dealt with by the French courts, whatever the letting agreement says.

c) **Law**

The tenancy will normally be governed by French law. It is possible for the parties to choose the law governing the contract, but the choice will be of limited effect as the mandatory requirements that the law of the country where the property is situated (France) will always apply irrespective of choice of law.

A.1   **ENGLISH-LANGUAGE AGREEMENT MADE SUBJECT MAINLY TO THE JURISDICTION OF THE COURTS OF ENGLAND AND WALES**

Agreement

BETWEEN

.... (the 'Landlord' or the Landlord's agents appointed for the purposes of managing the property in the absence of the Landlord)

AND

.... (the 'Tenant')

IT IS HEREBY AGREED AS FOLLOWS:

1.   In this Agreement the following terms have the following meanings:

   1.1   'The Property' means ....

   1.2   'The Contents' means the fixtures and fittings, furnishings, furniture and effects in the Property which are specified in the attached Inventory signed by both parties.

   1.3   'The Term' means the term of .... days/weeks/months.

   1.4   'The Commencement Date' means the .... day of .... 200.......

         at .... Hrs (local French time)

1.5 'The Termination Date' means the .... day of .... 200........

at .... Hrs (local French time)

1.6 'The Rent' means £................

1.7 'The Deposit' means a deposit of £................ payable to the Landlord in accordance with clause 6. below. The Deposit paid does not constitute arrhes or a dédit and the parties waive the provisions of Article 1590 of the French Civil Code

2. The Landlord agrees to let and the Tenant agrees to take the Property together with the Contents for the Term commencing on the Commencement Date and terminating on the Termination Date at the Rent to be paid, of which £................ is to be paid on the date hereof and the balance of £................ is to be paid not less than ... weeks before The Commencement Date

3. The tenant hereby covenants:

3.1 To pay the Rent on the days and in the manner aforesaid

3.2 To pay and indemnify the Landlord against all rates and assessments of an annual and for all water, gas and electricity consumed or supplied to the Property and all charges for the use of the telephone (if any) at the Property during the Term and any permitted continuation thereof or a proper proportion of the amount of any such charges to be assessed according to the duration of the Term

3.3 To keep:

3.3.1 the interior of the Property clean and tidy (including but not limited to the painting, decoration and papering thereof) and

3.3.2 all those parts of the Property in as good and tenantable state of repair and condition as at the beginning of the Term reasonable wear and tear and damage by fire excepted

3.4 To use the Property in a Tenant-like manner

3.5 To keep the Contents clean, in good repair and condition and maintain all electrical and mechanical equipment in good working order (reasonable wear and tear and damage by fire excepted) and replace immediately any broken windows at the Property and from time to time replace any of the Contents which may be broken, lost, destroyed or so damaged by the Tenant, his family, servants or agents as to be unusable with others of similar value and appearance

3.6   Not to cause or suffer any damage or injury to be done to the Property by the Tenant, his family, servants or agents

3.7   To notify the Landlord forthwith in writing (except in the case of emergency) of any defect in the Property other than such as the tenant is liable to remedy under Clause 3.3 above as soon as practical after such defect comes to the notice of the Tenant

3.8   To permit the Landlord or his agents at reasonable hours in the daytime by appointment (except in the case of an emergency) to enter the Property to view their state and condition and that of the Contents, to take inventories and to execute repairs and other necessary works upon the Property or any part of the building of which the Property forms part, or any adjoining or adjacent building, and permit the Landlord or his agents to give notice to the Tenant of all dilapidations, wants of repair, cleansing, painting, restoration to the interior of the Property then found and of all such breakage, loss, destruction or damage of or to the Contents, as the Tenant shall be bound to make good then found and by such notice to require the Tenant to repair, cleanse, paint, restore or make good the same within .... days/weeks from the service of such notice and if the Tenant fails by himself, his servants or agents to execute the said work within the said period permit the Landlord to enter upon the Property to execute the said work at the tenants expense

3.9   Not to make any alteration or addition to the Property or to paint, decorate or paper any part of the Property without first obtaining the Landlord's written consent to either the alterations or additions or the colour schemes for the painting, decoration and papering of the Property

3.10 To clean both sides of all windows at the Property as often as may be necessary

3.11 Not to remove, permit, cause or suffer to be removed any of the Contents from the Property or from the respective positions in the Property which they occupy at the commencement of the Term

3.12 Not at any time to bring onto the Property or any part a waterbed of any description whatsoever nor permit or cause or suffer any heavy objects to be brought onto the Property or any part thereof

3.13 Not to carry on, permit, cause or suffer to be carried on any trade, profession or study upon the Property nor receive paying guests but to use the Property only as a single private residence

3.14 Not to exhibit, permit, cause or suffer to be exhibited any poster or notice so as to be visible from the exterior of the Property

3.15 Not to permit, cause or suffer to be done on the Property anything which may be or become a nuisance or annoyance to the Landlord or the occupiers of any adjoining premises or which may render the Landlord's insurance of the Property void or voidable or increase the rate of premium for such insurance

3.16 Not to use, permit, cause or suffer the Property to be used for any illegal or immoral purpose

3.17 Not to make any noise or play any radio or television set or hi-fi or other music system or musical instrument in or about the Property between 23.00 hours and 07.00 hours so as to be audible outside the Property nor permit, cause or suffer the same

3.18 Not to block or cause any blockage to the drains, pipes, gutters, channels in or about the Property

3.19 Not to assign, sublet, share or part with possession or cease to occupy the whole or any part of the Property

3.20 Not to sell, charge or share possession of the Contents whether collectively or individually

3.21 Not to keep, permit or suffer to be kept at the Property or any part thereof without the Landlord's prior written consent any animal whether of a domestic nature or otherwise

3.22 To permit the Landlord or his agents at reasonable hours by appointment to enter the Property at any time during the Term with prospective tenants or purchasers of the Landlord's interest in the Property

3.23 At the Termination Date:

3.23.1 To yield up the Property and Contents any any articles substituted for the same in such state of repair and condition as shall be in accordance with the Tenant's obligations under this agreement

3.23.2 To pay for the washing (including ironing and pressing) of all linen, counterpanes, blankets etc (if any) and for the cleaning of all curtains which have been soiled during the Term

3.23.3 To make good or pay for the repair or replacements of such of the Contents as have been broken, lost or damaged during the Term or any continuation thereof (reasonable wear and tear and any damage by fire excepted)

3.24 To pay the costs of and incidental to the grant of this Agreement

3.25 Not by himself, his family, servant or agents to lop, top, cut down, remove or otherwise injure any trees, shrubs or plants growing at the Property or alter the general character of the garden but to keep the garden clean, tidy and in a proper state of cultivation according to the season of the year

4. The Landlord covenants that he will:

4.1 Permit the Tenant so long as he pays the rent and performs his obligations under this Agreement quietly to use and enjoy the Property during the Term without any interruption from the Landlord or any person rightfully claiming under or in trust for the Landlord

4.2 Keep in repair the structure and exterior of the Property (including the drains, gutters and external pipes) and insured against damage by fire

4.3 Keep in repair and proper working order the installations in the Property

4.3.1 for the supply of water, gas and electricity and for sanitation (including basins, sinks, baths and sanitary conveniences but not the fixtures and appliances for making use of the supply of water, gas or electricity) and

4.3.2 for space heating or heating water

4.4 This term shall not be construed as requiring the Landlord

4.4.1 to carry out any works or repairs for which the Tenant is liable by virtue of his duty to use the Property in a tenant-like manner

4.4.2 to rebuild or reinstate the Property in the case of destruction or damage by fire or by tempest, flood or other inevitable accident

4.4.3 to keep in repair or maintain anything which the Tenant is entitled to remove from the Property

4.5 In determining the standard of repair required by this Agreement regard shall be had to the age, character and prospective life of the Property and locality in which it is situated

4.6 Return to the Tenant any Rent payable for any period during which the Property may have been rendered uninhabitable by fire or any other risk against which the Landlord has insured

5. PROVIDED ALWAYS that, if at any time during the Term the Tenant fails to observe any of the stipulations in clause 3 hereof the Landlord may at any time thereafter re-enter upon the Property or any part thereof in the name of the whole and thereupon the tenancy granted shall absolutely determine but without prejudice to any claim of the Landlord in respect of any breach of the stipulations contained in clause 3 hereof

5.1 The Landlord acknowledges receipt from the Tenant of the Deposit on account of the Tenants obligations under clause 3 hereof which may be applied by the Landlord towards the cost of carrying out any works to the Property and/or for damage or breakage or repair to any of the Contents whether during the Term or at the Date of Termination

5.2 The Landlord agrees to repay the same to the Tenant within four weeks of the Date of Termination without interest after the deduction for any sums specified in clause 6.1

6. For the avoidance of doubt the Tenant is responsible for insuring his own contents and personal effects kept in the Property for the duration of this Agreement

7. IT IS AGREED AND DECLARED

7.1 That repossession proceedings and other matters directly affecting the Property shall be governed by French law and shall be subject to the exclusive jurisdiction of the French courts. All other matters concerning compliance with this Agreement shall be governed by English law and shall be submitted to the exclusive jurisdiction of the courts of England and Wales.

7.2 That prior to the execution of this Agreement the Tenant has read and approved the contents of this Agreement

Signed by the Landlord . . . .

Address . . . .

Occupation . . . .

Signed by the Tenant ....

Address ....

Occupation ....

Appendix

a) Inventory

b) Schedule of condition

c) Lease of the common parts (if applicable)

A.2 FRENCH LANGUAGE HOLIDAY LETTING AGREEMENT MADE SUBJECT TO THE JURISDICTION OF THE FRENCH COURTS AND TO FRENCH LAW

Engagement de Location Meublée Saisonnière

Entre les soussignés: ....

dénommé(s) 'Le bailleur' en singulier

Mandataire (le cas échéant):

et ....

dénommé(s) 'Le locataire' en singulier

Le bailleur et le locataire ont convenu et arrêté ce qui suit:

Le bailleur loue au locataire qui accepte, à titre de location saisonnière, les locaux meublés ci-après désignés

1. Désignation des locaux

Adresse: ....

Type de logement: Appartement/Bungalow/Villa/Chalet/Maison individuelle

Surface: .... m^2

Nombre de pièces:

tel que désigné dans l'état descriptif remis avant la rédaction de la présente location au locataire qui le reconnaît, et dont un exemplaire est annexé au contrat.

2. Conditions particulières

La présente location est consentie aux conditions générales figurant au Paragraphe 3, ainsi qu'aux conditions définies ci-après.

2.1 Durée

La présente location est consentie pour une durée de: ....

Entrée: le .... à .... h .... Sortie: le .... à .... h ....

2.2 Loyer TTC (cf 3.5)

	Sommes en toutes lettres	Sommes en chiffres
Loyer:	.... €	.... €
Charges:	.... €	.... €
Taxes:	.... €	.... €

2.3 Taxe de séjour

.... €   .... €

(par personne et par jour)

2.4 Réservation (cf 3.3 et 3.4)

(a) Locaux classés:

Arrhes .... €   .... €

(b) Locaux non classés:

.... €   .... €

Arrhes ou acompte

2.5 Nettoyage: .... €   .... €

2.6 Honoraires: (le cas échéant)

......................€   ....€

Les honoraires sont à la charge du

Honoraires de location: ....€

Frais d'état des lieux et d'inventaire: ....€

Frais de dossier: ....€

Total: ....€

2.7 Documents annexés:

(a) Etat des lieux contradictoire

(b) Etat descriptif détaillé du logement

(c) Inventaire du mobilier

(d) En cas de location classée: Tableau de classement des locations

2.8 Couchage: Le couchage est prévu pour un nombre maximum de personnes fixé à: ....

2.9 Dispositions complémentaires:

2.10 Remise des clés: Personne à contacter: M ....

3. Conditions générales

3.1 Régime juridique du contrat

La présente location est conclue à titre de résidence provisoire et de plaisance.

Les locaux ne pourront être utilisés à titre d'habitation principale ou même secondaire et le locataire ne pourra y pratiquer aucune activité commerciale, artisanale ou professionnelle.

En conséquence, le contrat sera régi par les dispositions du Code Civil ainsi que par les conditions prévues aux présentes. En cas de contestation, compétence exclusive est attribuée aux Tribunaux Français.

3.2　Durée

Le bail cesse de plein droit à l'expiration du terme fixé (cf 2.1), sans qu'il soit nécessaire de donner congé. La location ne pourra être prorogée sans l'accord préalable et écrit du bailleur.

3.3　Formation du contrat

(a)　Réservation par le locataire

Le locataire effectuant une réservation signe et renvoie au bailleur le contrat accompagné IMPERATIVEMENT du montant de la réservation indiqué au 2.4.

Le solde de la location reste payable à la remise des clefs DES L'ARRIVEE.

(b)　Confirmation par le bailleur ou son mandataire

Dans un délai de 10 jours à compter de la réception du chèque de réservation, le bailleur ou son mandataire fait un courrier:

● soit confirmant au locataire la disponibilité des locaux, l'engagement des parties devenant ferme;

● soit restituant au locataire intégralement la somme versée, les locaux choisis par le locataire n'étant plus disponibles pour la période souhaitée.

Sur demande expresse du locataire, le bailleur ou son mandataire pourra conserver cette somme pour la location d'un local similaire ou pour une autre période, les conditions de cette nouvelle location étant immédiatement transmises au locataire en vue de recueillir son accord exprès.

(c)　Nature de l'engagement

Lorsque la somme versée pour la réservation est qualifiée d'acompte, l'engagement du bailleur et du locataire est DEFINITIF.

En conséquence, si l'une des parties refuse d'exécuter ses obligations, l'autre partie peut en demander l'exécution forcée de la réparation.

3.4   Annulation du contrat, le cas échéant

C'est seulement lorsque la somme versée pour la réservation constitue des arrhes que le locataire ou le bailleur peut se dédire aux conditions suivantes:

- le locataire en abandonnant au bailleur la somme versée;

- le bailleur en retournant au locataire le double de la somme reçue.

3.5 Loyer – Dépôt de garantie

Les montants du loyer, des taxes (droit de bail, taxe de séjour...) et charges éventuelles et du dépôt de garantie sont indiqués aux paragraphes 2.2, 2.3, 2.4, 2.5 et 2.6.

Dès son arrivée, à la remise des clés, le locataire versera entre les mains du bailleur une somme dont le montant est défini à 2.3, à titre de dépôt de garantie, pour répondre des dégâts qui pourraient être causés aux objets mobiliers ou autres garnissant les lieux loués.

Tout objet perdu, cassé, détérioré ou abîmé devra être remplacé ou remboursé au bailleur à sa valeur de remplacement par le locataire qui s'y oblige.

Ce dépôt de garantie, non productif d'intérêts, ne pourra en aucun cas être considéré comme le paiement d'une partie du loyer. Ce versement ne constitue pas des arrhes ni de dédit. En conséquence, les parties renoncent à se prévaloir des dispositions de l'article 1590 du Code Civil.

Il sera remboursé après restitution des clés et après déduction, s'il y a lieu, des réparations locatives, au départ du locataire ou au plus tard dans les 60 jours de son départ (arrêté du 8 janvier 1993).

Une somme forfaitaire sera éventuellement retenue pour le nettoyage des locaux; son montant est défini aux conditions particulières figurant à 2.6.

la restitution des clés au bailleur, en fin de location, n'emporte pas renonciation du bailleur à des indemnités pour réparations locatives, s'il prouve que les dommages sont le fait du locataire.

3.6   Couchage

Les locaux faisant l'objet de la présente location ne doivent, sous aucun prétexte, être occupés par un nombre de personnes supérieur à celui indiqué aux conditions particulières, sauf accord préalable et écrit du bailleur.

Le cas échéant, le bailleur pourra réclamer un supplément de loyer, ou refuser l'entrée dans les lieux.

3.7   Assurance

Le locataire doit être assuré à une compagnie d'assurances notoirement connue contre les risques de vol, incendie et dégât des eaux, tant pour ses risques locatifs que pour le mobilier donné en location, ainsi que pour les recours des voisins, et en justifier à première réquisition du bailleur.

En conséquence, ce dernier décline toute responsabilité pour le recours que sa compagnie d'assurance pourrait exercer contre le locataire en cas de sinistre.

3.8   Obligations principales du locataire

Il est tenu de

(a)   N'occuper les lieux que bourgeoisement, à l'exclusion de l'exercice de tout commerce, profession ou industrie, le locataire reconnaissant que cette location ne lui est consentie QU'A TITRE DE RESIDENCE PROVISOIRE ET DE PLAISANCE, condition majeure sans laquelle la présente location ne lui aurait pas été consentie.

(b)   Ne rien faire qui, de son fait ou du fait de sa famille ou de ses relations, puisse nuire à la tranquillité du voisinage ou des autres occupants.

(c)   En cas de location dans un immeuble collectif, se conformer en qualité d'occupant des lieux, au règlement intérieur de l'immeuble, dont il prendra connaissance par VOIE D'AFFICHAGE ou sur COMMUNICATION DU BAILLEUR.

(d)   Occuper les lieux personnellement et ne pouvoir EN AUCUN CAS sous-louer-même gratuitement, ni céder ses droits à la présente location, sauf accord écrit du bailleur.

(e) Ne pouvoir sous aucun prétexte entreposer des meubles meublants, exception faite pour le linge et menus objets.

(f) Ne faire aucune modification ni changement dans la disposition des meubles et des lieux.

(g) N'introduire aucun animal familial (chiens, chats...) dans les locaux loués sans autorisation préalable et écrit du bailleur, la possibilité de détention étant subordonnée au fait que l'animal ne cause aucun dégât à l'immeuble, ni aucun trouble de jouissance dans le voisinage.

(h) Laisser exécuter pendant la location, dans les lieux loués, les travaux dont l'urgence manifeste ne permet pas leur report.

(i) Entretenir les lieux loués, et les rendre en bon état de propreté et de réparations locatives en fin de jouissance.

(j) Informer immédiatement le bailleur de tout sinistre et des dégradations se produisant dans les lieux loués, même s'il n'en résulte aucun dommage apparent.

(k) Répondre des dégradations et pertes qui arrivent par son propre fait ou par le fait des personnes de sa maison, pendant la jouissance du local, à moins qu'il ne prouve qu'elles ont eu lieu sans sa faute ni celle des personnes susdésignées.

(l) Prévenir à l'avance du jour et de l'heure de son arrivée.

(m) PRENDRE RENDEZ-VOUS POUR LES FORMALITES DE SORTIE TROIS JOURS AVANT SON DEPART.

3.9 Obligations principales du bailleur

Il est tenu de:

(a) Délivrer les lieux loués en bon état d'usage et de réparations, ainsi que les équipements mentionnés au contrat en bon état de fonctionnement.

(b) Assurer au locataire la jouissance paisible des lieux loués et le garantir des vices et défauts de nature à y faire obstacle.

(c) Entretenir les locaux en état de servir à l'usage prévu.

(d)   Sauf urgence manifeste, ne pas effectuer de travaux dans les lieux loués pendant la durée de la location; tous travaux entraîneront dédommagement du locataire, pour les troubles de jouissance subis.

(e)   En cas de location dans un immeuble collectif, COMMUNIQUER au locataire le règlement intérieur de l'immeuble ou l'AFFICHER DANS LES PARTIES COMMUNES DE L'IMMEUBLE.

3.10   Election de domicile

Pour l'exécution des présentes, les parties font élection de domicile à l'immeuble en France.

4.   Informations pratiques

4.1   Comment réserver?

Le candidat locataire devra renvoyer le présent contrat dûment signé et accompagné de la somme demandée pour la réservation. **Attention!** S'il s'agit d'une location classée, cette somme constitue des arrhes; s'il s'agit d'une location non classée, cette somme est, au choix des parties, soit un acompte, soit des arrhes.

4.2   Organisation de l'arrivée

Le locataire devra prévenir à l'avance du jour, ainsi que de l'heure approximative de son arrivée, et faire en sorte de se présenter les jours ouvrables.

A la remise des clés, le solde de la location ainsi que le montant du dépôt de garantie prévus lui seront demandés.

4.3   Organisation du départ

Sauf accord préalable du bailleur, les locaux devront être libérés au plus tard pour le jour et l'heure prévus au 2.1.

4.4   Etat des lieux et inventaire du mobilier

L'état des lieux et l'inventaire détaillé du mobilier sont établis contradictoirement entre les parties à l'entrée dans les lieux du locataire et à la libération des locaux par le locataire, **sur rendez-vous préalable**.

Le cas échéant, le locataire a un délai de 3 jours pour contester l'état des lieux lors de son arrivée ou de son départ.

S'il n'a pas été fait l'état des lieux, le locataire est présumé avoir reçu les lieux loués en bon état de réparations locatives et doit les rendre tels sauf la preuve contraire (Article 1731 du Code Civil).

5. Signature des parties

Mots rayés:

Lignes rayées:

Fait et signé à .... le .... en ....
originaux dont un remis à chacune des parties qui le reconnaît.

Le bailleur ou son mandataire ....
(signature précédée de la mention manuscrite 'lu et approuvé')

Le(s) Locataire(s) ....
(signature précédée de la mention manuscrite 'lu et approuvé)

ATTENTION

Veuillez signer et dater séparement chaque exemplaire

A.3 FRENCH FURNISHED LETTING AGREEMENT FOR A DURATION OF SIX MONTHS OR LONGER

Contrat de location meublée à usage d'habitation secondaire

Exclu du champ d'application de la loi n° 89-462 du 6 juillet 1989

Entre les soussignés: ....

dénommé(s) 'Le Bailleur' en singulier

Mandataire (le cas échéant):

et ....

dénommé(s) 'Le Locataire' en singulier

Il a été convenu et arrêté ce qui suit:

Le Bailleur loue les locaux et équipements ci-après désignés au Locataire qui les accepte aux conditions suivantes:

1. Locaux

   Adresse:

   Consistance: Appartement/maison individuelle

   Dépendances:

   Garage n°

   Place de stationnement n°

   Cave n°

   Désignation des locaux et équipements privatifs:

   Enumération des parties et équipements communs:

   Gardiennage

   Interphone

   Ascenseur

   Vide-ordures

   Antenne T.V. collective

   Espace(s) vert(s)

   Chauffage collectif

   Eau chaude collective

2. Régime juridique

   En cas de contestation, compétence exclusive est attribuée aux Tribunaux Français.

   Le présent contrat de location est régi par les dispositions des articles 1714 à 1762 du Code Civil relatives aux baux d'immeubles à usage d'habitation ainsi que par les conditions prévues aux pages suivantes. Conclu dans le cadre de l'une des exclusions prévues à l'article 2 de la loi n° 89-462 du 6 juillet 1989, il n'est soumis ni aux dispositions de cette loi ni à celles prévues par la loi n° 48-1360 du 1 septembre 1948.

En conséquence, la durée du présent contrat de location ainsi que le montant du loyer sont librement fixés entre les parties.

Outre les conditions générales, le présent contrat de location est consenti et accepté aux prix, charges et conditions suivantes:

3. Durée du contrat (cf Conditions Générales Chapitre I):

    Le présent contrat est conclu pour une durée de .... renouvelable ensuite par tacite reconduction et par périodes de faute de congé préalable.

4. Date de prise d'effet

    Le contrat prendra effet le ....

5. Montant des paiements (cf Conditions Générales Chapitres III et IV)

    Loyer mensuel (somme en toutes lettres): .... €

    Taxe (droit de bail): .... €

    Charges mensuelles: .... €

    Total mensuel: .... €

6. Termes de paiement

    Cette somme sera payable d'avance et en totalité le .... de chaque mois, entre les mains du Bailleur, soit de ....

7. Révision du loyer (cf Conditions Générales Chapitre III)

    Le loyer sera révisé chaque année le ....

    Indice de référence: ....

    Trimestre 200........

    Valeur:

8. Dépôt de garantie (cf Conditions Générales Chapitre V)

    Cette somme (en toutes lettres) correspond à .... mois de loyer.

9. Clause particulière (le cas échéant)

10. Honoraires (le cas échéant, cf Conditions Générales Chapitre XII)

Honoraires de négociations: . . . .€

Honoraires de rédaction: . . . .€

Frais d'état des lieux: . . . .€

Total: . . . .€

Conformément aux usages locaux, ces frais seront à la charge du Bailleur/Locataire.

11. Documents annexés

Etat des lieux établi lors de la remise des clés au Locataire (contradictoire ou par huissier).

Liste des réparations locatives fixées par le décret n° 87-712 du 26 août 1987.

Liste des charges récupérables fixées par le décret n° 87-713 du 26 août 1987.

Inventaire du mobilier

Acte de caution solidaire, le cas échéant.

12. Clés remises

Nombre de clés remises au locataire:

13. Signature des parties

Mots rayés:

Lignes rayées:

Fait et signé à .... le .... en .... originaux dont un remis à chacune des parties qui le reconnaît.

Le Bailleur ou son Mandataire:

(Signature précédée de la mention manuscrite 'lu et approuvé')

Le Locataire:

(Signature précédée de la mention manuscrite 'lu et approuvé.')

La Caution

(Signature précédée de la mention manuscrite ' lu et approuvé. Je reconnais avoir reçu un exemplaire du présent contrat pour lequel je me pose caution par acte séparé et annexé.')

CONDITIONS GÉNÉRALES

I. **Durée (la date du contrat et sa date de prise d'effet sont indiquées en page 3)**

La durée du contrat, indiquée en page ...., est librement fixée entre les parties.

Si le logement faisant l'objet de la présente location est loué ou attribué en raison de l'exercice d'une fonction ou de l'occupation d'un emploi, la durée du présent contrat sera indissociable de celle du contrat de travail. En conséquence, si le contrat de travail vient à être dénoncé ou rompu, la présente location sera automatiquement résiliée dans les mêmes conditions.

II. *Résiliation*

Le contrat pourra être résilié par lettre recommandée avec avis de réception ou par acte d'huissier:

● Par le Locataire, à tout moment, en prévenant le bailleur trois mois à l'avance, délai ramené à un mois en cas de mutation, de perte d'emploi ou de nouvel emploi consécutif à une perte d'emploi.

● Par le Bailleur, en prévenant le Locataire trois mois avant le terme du contrat ou avant le terme de chacune des tacites reconductions.

III. *Loyer*

Le montant du loyer, librement fixé entre les parties, sera payable au domicile du Bailleur ou de la personne qu'il aurait mandatée à cet effet. Il sera révisé chaque année en fonction de l'indice national I.N.S.E.E. du coût de la construction dont les éléments de référence sont indiqués en page 3.

IV. *Charges*

En sus du loyer, le Locataire remboursera au Bailleur sa quote-part dans les charges réglementaires, conformément à la liste fixée par le décret n° 87-713 du 26 août 1987.

Les charges récupérables, sommes accessoires au loyer principal, sont exigibles en contrepartie:

● des services rendus liés à l'usage des différents éléments de la chose louée;

● des dépenses d'entretien courant et des menues réparations sur les éléments d'usage commun de la chose louée;

● du droit de bail et des impositions qui correspondent à des services dont le Locataire profite directement.

Elles seront réglées mensuellement, en même temps que le loyer principal.

Contrat d'une durée supérieure à un an:

Si le présent contrat est conclu pour une durée supérieure à un an, les charges mensuelles fixées en page 3 seront considérées comme des provisions devant faire l'objet d'une régularisation au moins annuelle.

Leur montant sera fixé chaque année par le Bailleur en fonction des dépenses réellement exposées l'année précédente ou du budget prévisionnel, le montant de chaque provision étant réajusté en conséquence.

Un mois avant l'échéance de la régularisation annuelle, le Bailleur adressera au Locataire un décompte par nature de charges ainsi que, dans les immeubles collectifs, le mode de répartition entre tous les locataires. Pendant ce mois, les pièces justificatives seront tenues à la disposition du Locataire.

Contrat d'une durée maximale d'un an

Par accord exprès entre les parties et dans un souci de simplification, si le présent contrat est conclu pour une durée maximale d'un an, les montants mensuels fixés en page 3 seront considérés comme des charges forfaitaires, apurant au fur et à mesure ce compte d'une façon définitive.

Cependant, si le contrat par le jeu de la tacite reconduction vient à dépasser la durée d'une année, dès ce seuil franchi, les charges devront être justifiées.

Les versements seront alors considérés comme des provisions devant faire l'objet de la régularisation annuelle selon les modalités prévues ci-avant pour les contrats d'une durée supérieure à un an.

V. **Dépôt de garantie**

Le dépôt de garantie éventuellement versé par le Locataire afin de garantir la bonne exécution de ses obligations est équivalent à la période de loyer indiquée en page 4 et sera modifié de plein droit à chaque augmentation de loyer de manière à demeurer équivalent à cette période.

Ce dépôt, non productif d'intérêts, est indépendant des loyers et charges, lesquels devront être régulièrement payés aux dates fixées, jusqu'au départ effectif du Locataire. (Le départ étant entendu après complet déménagement, exécution des réparations locatives, résiliation des abonnements de gaz, électricité, eau et téléphone, présentation au Bailleur de la quittance taxe d'habitation, établissement de l'état des lieux contradictoire en fin de contrat et remise des clés).

Il sera restitué au Locataire en fin de jouissance, dans le mois suivant l'envoi par le syndic du relevé des comptes de charges de la période intéressée, déduction faite, le cas échéant, des sommes dûment justifiées restant dues au Bailleur ou dont celui-ci pourrait être tenu pour responsable aux lieux et place du Locataire.

VI.   Etat des lieux (annexé au contrat)

Un état des lieux contradictoire sera établi lors de la remise des clés au Locataire et sera annexé aux présentes.

A défaut d'état des lieux, la présomption établie par l'article 1731 du Code Civil ne pourra être invoquée par celle des parties qui aura fait obstacle à l'établissement de l'état des lieux.

A la fin du contrat, lors de la restitution des clés par le Locataire, un état des lieux de sortie sera dressé contradictoirement entre les parties après rendez-vous pris avec le Bailleur huit jours à l'avance, à des heures ouvrables.

VII.   Obligations du Bailleur

Le Bailleur est tenu des obligations principales suivantes:

1. Délivrer au Locataire le logement en bon état d'usage et de réparations, ainsi que les équipements mentionnés au contrat en bon état de fonctionnement.

2. Assurer au Locataire la jouissance paisible du logement et, sans préjudice des dispositions de l'article 1721 du Code Civil, le garantir des vices de construction ou du bon fonctionnement des équipements.

VIII.   Obligations du Locataire

Le Locataire est tenu des obligations principales suivantes:

1. Payer le loyer et les charges récupérables aux termes convenus. Le paiement mensuel est de droit s'il en fait la demande.

2. User PAISIBLEMENT les locaux et équipements loués suivant la destination prévue au contrat.

3. Répondre des dégradations et pertes survenant pendant la durée du contrat dans les locaux dont il a la jouissance exclusive, à moins qu'il ne prouve qu'elles ont eu lieu par cas de force majeure, par la faute du Bailleur, ou par le fait d'un tiers qu'il n'a pas introduit dans le logement.

4. Prendre à sa charge l'entretien courant du logement et des équipements mentionnés au contrat, les menues réparations et l'ensemble des réparations locatives définies par le décret n° 87-712 du 26 août 1987, sauf si elles sont occasionnées par vétusté, malfaçon, vice de construction, cas forfait ou force majeure.

5. Souscrire un contrat d'entretien auprès d'une entreprise spécialisée (ou en rembourser le coût au Bailleur si ce dernier en assure le paiement) pour faire entretenir au moins une fois par an les équipements individuels (chauffage, gaz, brûleurs gaz...) et en justifier à première demande du Bailleur.

6. Informer immédiatement le Bailleur de tout sinistre et des dégradations se produisant dans les lieux loués, même s'il n'en résulte aucun dommage apparent.

7. Ne pas transformer sans l'accord écrit du Bailleur les locaux loués et leurs équipements: le Bailleur pourra, si le Locataire a méconnu cette obligation, exiger la remise en état des locaux et des équipements au départ du locataire ou conserver les transformations effectuées sans que le Locataire puisse réclamer une indemnité pour les frais engagés. Le Bailleur aura toutefois la faculté d'exiger aux frais du Locataire la remise immédiate des lieux en l'état si les transformations mettent en péril le bon fonctionnement des équipements ou la sécurité du local.

8. Laisser exécuter dans les lieux loués les travaux d'amélioration des parties communes ou des parties privatives du même immeuble, ainsi que les travaux nécessaires au maintien et état et à l'entretien normal des locaux loués: les dispositions des deuxième et troisième aliénas de l'article 1724 du Code Civil étant applicables à ces travaux.

9. Ne faire installer et ne faire usage d'aucun nouveau système de chauffage sans avoir vérifié à ses frais, et sous sa responsabilité, la conformité des cheminées avec les règles de sécurité en vigueur.

Faire le ramonage des cheminées à ses frais, au moins une fois l'an et en fin de jouissance.

10. Respecter le règlement intérieur de l'immeuble affiché dans les parties communes des immeubles collectifs.

Se conformer à toutes demandes ou instructions pouvant être formulées par le Bailleur en vertu des décisions d'assemblées générales des copropriétaires ou du règlement intérieur de l'immeuble et en exécuter strictement toutes les dispositions.

11. S'assurer contre les risques locatifs dont il doit répondre en sa qualité de Locataire: incendie, dégât des eaux etc, et en justifier au Bailleur à la remise des clés, en lui transmettant l'attestation émise par son assureur ou son représentant. Il devra en justifier ainsi chaque année, à la demande du Bailleur.

12. Occuper personnellement les lieux loués; ne pas céder le contrat de location, ni sous-louer le logement sauf avec accord écrit du Bailleur, y compris sur le prix du loyer. En cas de cessation du contrat principal, le sous-locataire ne pourra se prévaloir d'aucun droit à l'encontre du Bailleur, ni d'aucun titre d'occupation.

13. Laisser visiter, en vue de la vente ou de la location, les lieux loués deux heures par jour pendant les jours ouvrables. L'horaire de visite sera défini par accord entre les parties: à défaut d'accord, les visites auront lieu entre 17 h et 19 h.

14. Répondre de la perte ou de la détérioration des meubles mis à sa disposition par le Bailleur et dont l'inventaire est joint aux présentes; s'interdire absolument de transporter le mobilier hors des lieux loués.

15. Ne pas déménager, sans être conformé à ses obligations (paiement des loyers, des charges et des contributions diverses lui incombant personnellement, relevé des différents compteurs, exécution des réparations locatives etc), ni sans avoir auparavant présenté au Bailleur les quittances justifiant du paiement de la taxe d'habitation.

16. Remettre au Bailleur, dès son départ, toutes les clés des locaux loués et lui faire connaître sa nouvelle adresse.

IX.   *Clause résolutoire et clauses pénales*

Le présent contrat sera RESILIE IMMEDIATEMENT ET DE PLEIN DROIT un mois après un commandement demeuré infructueux, sans qu'il soit besoin de faire ordonner cette résolution en justice, dans les cas suivants:

● à défaut de paiement aux termes convenus de tout ou partie du loyer et des charges;

● en cas de non versement du dépôt de garantie éventuellement prévu au contrat;

● en cas d'inexécution de l'une quelconque des conditions du présent contrat, qui sont toutes de rigueur;

- à défaut d'assurance contre les risques locatifs ou à défaut de justification au bailleur à chaque période convenue.

Une fois acquis au Bailleur le bénéfice de la clause résolutoire, le locataire devra libérer immédiatement les lieux; s'il refuse, son expulsion aura lieu sur simple ordonnance de référé.

Il est bien entendu qu'en cas de paiement par chèque, le loyer ne sera considéré comme réglé qu'après encaissement.

En outre, et sans qu'il soit dérogé à la précédente clause résolutoire, le Locataire s'engage formellement à respecter les deux clauses pénales qui suivent:

1. En cas de non paiement du loyer ou de ses accessoires aux termes convenus, et dès le premier acte d'huissier, le Locataire supportera une majoration de plein droit de 10% sur le montant des sommes dues, en dédommagement du préjudice subi par le Bailleur, et ce sans qu'une mise en demeure soit nécessaire, en dérogation à l'article 1230 du Code Civil.

2. Si le Locataire déchu de tout droit d'occupation ne libère pas les lieux, résiste à une ordonnance d'expulsion ou obtient des délais pour son départ, il devra verser par jour de retard, outre les charges, une indemnité conventionnelle d'occupation égale à deux fois le loyer quotidien, ceci jusqu'à complet déménagement et restitution des clés.

Cette indemnité est destinée à dédommager le Bailleur du préjudice provoqué par l'occupation abusive des lieux loués faisant obstacle à l'exercice des droits du Bailleur.

X. *Tolérances*

Il est formellement convenu que toutes les tolérances de la part du Bailleur, relatives aux conditions énoncées ci-dessus, qu'elles qu'en aient été la fréquence et la durée, ne pourront en aucun cas être considérées comme apportant une modification ou suppression de ces conditions, ni génératrices d'un droit quelconque. Le Bailleur pourra toujours y mettre fin à tout moment.

XI. *Solidarité – Indivisibilité – Election de domicile*

Pour l'exécution de toutes les obligations résultant du présent contrat, il y aura solidarité et indivisibilité entre:

- les parties ci-dessus désignées sous le vocable 'le Locataire';

- les héritiers ou représentants du Locataire venant à décéder (sous réserve de l'article 802 du Code Civil).

Cependant le contrat sera résilié immédiatement et de plein droit en cas de décès du Locataire bénéficiant du logement en raison de l'exercice d'une profession ou de l'exécution d'un contrat de travail.

Les parties signataires font élection de domicile; le Bailleur en sa demeure et le Locataire des lieux loués.

XII.   *Frais – Honoraires*

Les honoraires éventuels de négociation et de rédaction des présentes ainsi que la ou les parties à qui en incombe la charge sont indiqués en page 4.

Les frais, droits et honoraires qui en seront la suite ou la conséquence, seront à la charge du Locataire qui s'y oblige. Il en sera de même pour les honoraires et frais consécutifs au recouvrement des loyers et charges par voie d'huissier ou de justice.

ANNEXE A

LISTE DE RÉPARATIONS LOCATIVES FIXÉES PAR LE DÉCRET N° 87-712 DU 26 AOÛT 1987

1. *Parties extérieures dont le Locataire à l'usage exclusif*

a) **Jardins privatifs**

Entretien courant, notamment des allées, pelouses, massifs, bassins et piscines; taille, échenillage des arbres et arbustes. Remplacement des arbustes; réparation et remplacement des installations mobiles d'arrosage.

b) **Auvents, terrasses et marquises**

Enlèvement de la mousse et des autres végétaux.

c) **Descentes d'eau pluviale, chéneaux et gouttières**

Dégorgement des conduits.

2. *Ouvertures intérieures et extérieures*

a) **Sections ouvrantes telles que portes et fenêtres**

Graissage des gonds, paumelles et charnières. Menues réparations des boutons et poignées de portes, des gonds, crémones et espagnolettes; remplacement notamment de boulons, clavettes et targettes.

b) **Vitrages**

Réfection des mastics. Remplacement des vitres détériorées.

c) **Dispositifs d'occulation de la lumière tels que stores et jalousies**

Graissage; remplacement notamment de cordes, poulies ou de quelques lames.

d) **Serrures et verrous de sécurité**

Graissage; remplacement de petites pièces ainsi que des clés égarées ou détériorées.

e) **Grilles**

Nettoyage et graissage; remplacement notamment de boulons, clavettes et targettes.

3. *Parties intérieures*

a) **Plafonds, murs intérieurs et cloisons**

Maintien en état de propreté; menus raccords de peintures et tapisseries; remise en place ou remplacement de quelques éléments des matériaux de revêtement tels que faïence, mosaïque, matière plastique; rebouchage des trous rendu assimilable à une réparation par le nombre, la dimension et l'emplacement de ceux-ci.

b) **Parquets, moquettes et autres revêtements de sol**

Encaustiquage et entretien courant de la vitrification; remplacement de quelques lames de parquets et remise en état, pose de raccords de moquettes et autres revêtements de sol, notamment en cas de taches et de trous.

c) **Placards et menuiseries telles que plinthes, baguettes et moulures**

Remplacement des tablettes et tasseaux de placard et réparation de leur dispositif de fermeture; fixation de raccords et remplacement de pointes de menuiseries.

4. *Installations de plomberie*

a) **Canalisations d'eau**

Dégorgement; remplacement notamment de joints et de colliers.

b) **Canalisations de gaz**

Entretien courant de robinets, siphons et ouvertures d'aération; remplacement périodique des tuyaux souples de raccordement. Vidange.

c) **Chauffage, production d'eau chaude et robinetterie**

Remplacement des bilames, pistons, membranes, boîtes à eau, allumage piézo-éléctrique, clapets et joints des appareils à gaz; rinçage et nettoyage des corps de chauffe et tuyauteries; remplacement des joints, clapets et presse-étoupes des robinets; remplacement des joints, flotteurs et joints closes des chasses d'eau.

d) **Eviers et appareils sanitaires**

Nettoyage des dépôts de calcaire, remplacement des tuyaux flexibles de douches.

5. *Equipement d'installations d'électricité*

Remplacement des interrupteurs, prises de courant, coupe-circuits et fusibles, des ampoules, tubes lumineux; réparation ou remplacement des baguettes ou gaines de protection.

6. *Autres équipements mentionnés au contrat de location*

a) Entretien courant et menues réparations des appareils tels que réfrigérateurs, machines à laver de linge et de vaisselle, sèche-linge, hottes aspirantes, adoucisseurs, capteurs solaires, pompes à chaleur, appareils de conditionnement d'air, antennes individuelles de radiodiffusion et de télévision, meubles scellés, cheminées, glaces et miroirs.

b) Menues réparations nécessitées par la dépose des bourrelets.

c) Graissage et remplacement des joints des vidoirs.

d) Ramonage des conduits d'évacuation des fumées et des gaz et conduits de ventilation.

ANNEXE B

LISTE DE CHARGES RÉCUPÉRABLES FIXÉES PAR LE DÉCRET N° 87-713 DU 26 AOÛT 1987

1. ASCENSEURS ET MONTE-CHARGE

1.1 Dépenses d'électricité

1.2 Dépenses d'exploitation, d'entretien courant, de menues réparations:

a) Exploitation

- visite périodique, nettoyage et graissage des organes mécaniques;

- examen semestriel des câbles et vérification annuelle des parachutes;

- nettoyage annuel de la cuvette, du dessus de la cabine et de la machinerie;

- dépannage ne nécessitant pas de réparations ou fournitures de pièces;

- tenue d'un dossier par l'entreprise d'entretien mentionnant les visites techniques, incidents et faits importants touchant l'appareil.

b) Fournitures relatives à des produits ou à du petit matériel d'entretien (chiffons, graisses et huiles nécessaires) et aux lampes d'éclairage de la cabine.

c) Menues réparations

- de la cabine (boutons d'envoi, paumelles de portes, contacts de portes, fermes-portes automatiques, coulisseaux de cabine, dispositif de sécurité de treuil et cellule photo-électriques);

- des paliers (ferme-portes mécaniques, électriques ou pneumatiques, serrures électromécaniques, contacts de porte et boutons d'appel);

- des balais du moteur et fusibles.

2. EAU FROIDE, EAU CHAUDE ET CHAUFFAGE COLLECTIF DES LOCAUX PRIVATIFS ET DES PARTIES COMMUNES

2.1 Dépenses relatives

A l'eau froide et chaude des locataires ou occupants du bâtiment ou de l'ensemble des bâtiments d'habitation concernés;

A l'eau nécessaire à l'entretien courant des parties communes du ou desdits bâtiments, y compris la station d'épuration;

A l'eau nécessaire à l'entretien courant des espaces extérieurs;

Les dépenses relatives à la consommation d'eau incluent l'ensemble des taxes et redevances ainsi que les sommes dues au titre de la redevance d'assainissement, à l'exclusion de celles auxquelles le propriétaire est astreint en application de l'article L.35-5 du Code de la Santé publique;

Aux produits nécessaires à l'exploitation, à l'entretien et au traitement de l'eau;

A l'électricité;

Au combustible ou à la fourniture, quelle que soit sa nature.

2.2 *Dépenses d'exploitation, d'entretien courant et de menues réparations*

a) **Exploitation et entretien courant:**

- nettoyage des gicleurs, électrodes, filtres et clapets des brûleurs;

- entretien courant et graissant des pompes de relais, jauges, contrôleurs de niveau ainsi que des groupes motopompes et pompes de puisards;

- graissage des vannes et robinets et réfection des presse- étoupes;

- remplacement des ampoules, des voyants lumineux et ampoules de chaufferie;

- entretien et réglage des appareils de régulation automatique et de leurs annexes;

- vérification et entretien des régulateurs de tirage;

- réglage des vannes, robinets et tés ne comprenant pas l'équilibrage;

- purge des points de chauffage;

- frais de contrôle de combustion;

- entretien des épurateurs de fumée;

- opérations de mise en repos en fin de saison de chauffage, rinçage des corps de chauffe et tuyauteries, nettoyage de chaufferies, y compris leurs puisards et siphons, ramonage des chaudières, carneaux et cheminées;

- conduite de chauffage;

- frais de location, d'entretien et de relevé des compteurs généraux et individuels;

- entretien de l'adoucisseur, du détartreur d'eau, du surpresseur et du détendeur;

- contrôles périodiques visant à éviter les fuites de fluide frigorigène des pompes de chaleur;

- vérification, nettoyage et graissage des organes des pompes à chaleur;

- nettoyage périodique de la face extérieure des capteurs solaires;

- vérification, nettoyage et graissage des organes des capteurs solaires.

b) **Menues réparations dans les parties communes ou sur des éléments d'usage commun:**

- réparation des fuites sur raccords et joints;

- remplacement des joints, clapets et presse-étoupes;

- rodage des sièges de clapets;

- menues réparations visant à remédier aux fuites de fluide frigorigène des pompes à chaleur;

- recharge en fluide frigorigène des pompes à chaleur.

3. **INSTALLATIONS INDIVIDUELLES**

Chauffage et production d'eau chaude, distribution d'eau dans les parties privatives:

3.1 Dépenses d'alimentation commune de combustible

3.2 Exploitation et entretien courant, menues réparations

a) Exploitation et entretien courant

- réglage de débit et température de l'eau chaude sanitaire;

- vérification et réglage des appareils de commande, d'asservissement, de sécurité d'aquastat et de pompe;

- dépannage;

- contrôle des raccordements et de l'alimentation des chauffe-eau électriques, contrôle de l'intensité absorbée;

- vérification de l'état des résistances, des thermostats, nettoyage;

- réglage des thermostats et contrôle de la température d'eau;

- contrôle et réfection d'étanchéité des raccordements eau froide eau chaude;

- contrôle des groupes de sécurité;

- rodage des sièges de clapets des robinets;

- réglage des mécanismes de chasses d'eau.

b) **Menues réparations**

- remplacement des bilames, pistons, membranes, boîtes à eau, allumage piézo-électrique, clapets et joints des appareils à gaz;

- rinçage et nettoyage des corps de chauffe et tuyauteries;

- remplacement des joints, clapets et presse-étoupes des robinets;

- remplacement des joints, flotteurs et joints cloches des chasses d'eau.

4. PARTIES COMMUNES INTÉRIEURES AU BÂTIMENT OU À L'ENSEMBLE DES BÂTIMENTS D'HABITATION

4.1 *Dépenses relatives*

- à l'électricité;

- aux fournitures consommables, notamment produits d'entretien, balais et petit matériel assimilé nécessaire à l'entretien de propreté, sel.

4.2 *Exploitation et entretien courant, menues réparations*

- entretien de la minuterie, pose, dépose et entretien des tapis;

- menues réparations des appareils d'entretien de propreté tels qu'aspirateur.

4.3 *Entretien de propreté (frais de personnel)*

5. ESPACES EXTÉRIEURS AU BÂTIMENT OU À L'ENSEMBLE DES BÂTIMENTS D'HABITATION (VOIES DE CIRCULATION, AIRES DE STATIONNEMENT, ABORDS ET ESPACES VERTS, AIRES ET ÉQUIPEMENTS DE JEUX).

5.1 Dépenses relatives

● à l'électricité;

● à l'essence et l'huile;

● aux fournitures consommables utilisées dans l'entretien courant: ampoules ou tubes d'éclairage, engrais, produits bactéricides et insecticides, produits tels que graines, fleurs, plants, plantes de remplacement, à l'exclusion de celles utilisées pour la réfection de massifs, plates-bandes ou haies.

5.2 Exploitation et entretien courant

Opérations de coupe, désherbage, sarclage, ratissage, nettoyage et arrosage concernant:

● les allées aires de stationnement et abords;

● les espaces verts (pelouses, massifs, arbustes, haies vives, plates-bandes);

● les aires de jeux;

● les bassins, fontaines, caniveaux, canalisations d'évacuation des eaux pluviales;

● entretien du matériel horticole;

● remplacement du sable des bacs et du petit matériel de jeux;

● peinture et menues réparations des bancs de jardin et des équipements de jeux et grillages.

6. HYGIÈNE

6.1 Dépenses de fournitures consommables

● sacs en plastique et en papier nécessaires à l'élimination des rejets;

● produits relatifs à la désinsectisation et à la désinfection, y compris des colonnes sèches de vide-ordures.

6.2 *Exploitation et entretien courant*

- entretien et vidange des fosses d'aisances;

- entretien des appareils de conditionnement des ordures.

6.3 *Elimination des rejets (frais de personnel)*

7. **EQUIPEMENT DIVERS DU BÂTIMENT OU DE L'ENSEMBLE DES BÂTIMENTS D'HABITATION**

7.1 *La fourniture nécessaire à la ventilation mécanique*

7.2 *Exploitation et entretien courant*

- ramonage des conduits de ventilation;

- entretien de la ventilation mécanique;

- entretien des dispositifs d'ouverture automatique ou codée et des interphones;

- visites périodiques à l'exception des contrôles réglementaires de sécurité, nettoyage et graissage de l'appareillage fixe de manutention des nacelles de nettoyage des façades vitrées.

7.3 *Divers*

- abonnement des postes de téléphone à la disposition des locataires.

8. **IMPOSITIONS ET REDEVANCES**

- taxe ou redevance d'enlèvement des ordures ménagères;

- taxe de balayage.

APPENDIX B: TYPICAL INCOME TAX COMPUTATIONS

TAX COMPUTATION A – Furnished holiday letting by non-residents

1. Mr and Mrs Frank O'File are non-French resident individuals who own a home in the Dordogne. The value of the property (buildings only) is €150,000. The property is in fact let out on a furnished basis from time to time and produced a rental income of €18,500 in 2001. The couple occupied the property for 1 month, for which the rental value is estimated at €730. They paid €915 in *taxes foncières,* €610 in *taxe d'habitation* and €610 for repairs and maintenance during the year. They have no other French sources of income, but substantial income from sources outside France. They are married with two minor children. Their country of residence has concluded a full double tax treaty with France (*Note 1*).

2. Because they are letting the property on a furnished basis, Mr & Mrs O'File's French source income will be assessed under business income rules and not as rental income. But since their rental income does not exceed €76,300, they will be assessed under the *Micro BIC* regime for calculation of their taxable income.

3. They will not be considered to be 'professional landlords' because their rental income is less than €23,000 per annum and it does not constitute the greater part of their income. Apart from certain consequences in terms of the availability of relief for any losses on the lettings, which are unlikely to concern Mr and Mrs O'File, the main consequence of not being 'professional landlords' is that any gain on an eventual disposal of the property will be taxed as a private capital gain and not as a business gain.

4. Theoretically, if they elected to have their business income calculated under the rules for the 'real' regime, the O'Files would still be able to claim depreciation on the buildings as a business expense, provided that the property was included in the balance sheet of the business. However if it were so included, they would have to declare a rent for the period that they occupied the property. On the assumptions that they choose to be assessed under the *Micro BIC* rules, their income tax liability for 2001, payable in 2002, will be computed as follows:

Income of 2001	€	€
Rental income (*Note 2*)		18,500
Less: Global deduction for expenses (70%)		12,950
		€5,550
Minimum income tax liability for non-residents at 25% (*Note 1*)		€1,388

Note 1. Because Mr & Mrs Frank O'File are resident in a country which has concluded a full double tax treaty with France, they are not subject to tax on a notional income of three times the annual rental value of the property. Correspondingly, however, their liability is subject to the minimum tax rate of 25%. If their liability calculated at scale rates exceeded the minimum liability, the normal scale rates would apply, but this will clearly not be the case in this example.

Note 2. Mr & Mrs Frank O'File are not liable to pay any social contributions because they are not resident in France.

Note 3. It does not matter whether the rent is paid to the couple by non-French residents or into a bank account outside France. The income is still French source income, and subject to tax in France.

5. *Mr & Mrs Frank O'File* would also pay the tax on leases (see 7.3.3).

6. Generally a business of furnished lettings is not subject to the business tax (*taxe professionnelle*), unless the local government authorities have resolved that such businesses should pay this tax. There are areas of France where the *taxe professionnelle* is levied on landlords of furnished lettings.

TAX COMPUTATION B – Unfurnished letting by non-residents

1. Mr and Mrs English are UK residents. They own a French property and intend on moving there when they retire. In the meantime, they are letting it on an unfurnished basis to a French family.

2. The property is over 15 years old. They are getting an annual rental income of €16,500. As the income exceeds €15,000, their French tax liability is computed following the normal *Foncier* regime, as follows:

Income of 2001	€	€
Gross rental income		16,500
Less: Expenses paid on behalf of the tenants and not refunded by them	910	
General allowance at 14% (basis 16,500 less 910)	2,183	
Maintenance expenses	800	
Taxes Foncières and contribution sur les revenus locatifs paid in 2001	1,020	
Mortgage interest	2,960	
Total deductible expenses		7,873
Net taxable income		8,627
Minimum income tax liability rate for non-residents at 25%		2,157

3. Mr and Mrs English would also pay the tax on leases as their income exceeds €1,830 and their property is over 15 years old (see 7.3.3), this tax liability would be calculated as follows:

	€	€
Gross rental income		16,500
Less: Expenses (see above)	910	
Net taxable		15,590
Contribution sur les revenus locatifs at 2.5%		390

4. The tenants should normally pay the *taxe d'habitation*. If this is not the case Mr and Mrs English may deduct it from their taxable income as an expense paid on behalf of the tenants.

APPENDIX C:

FRENCH-ENGLISH GLOSSARY FOR HOME BUYERS AND HOME OWNERS

abandonner	to quit/surrender	acquis	acquired/vested
abat-jour	lampshade	acquittement	acquittal/discharge
abattant	desk/table flap/leaf	acte de vente	deed of sale
abattement	allowance/rebate	acte notarié	notarised deed
abîmer	to damage/to spoil	acte sous seing	private written
abolir	to cancel	privé	agreement
abonnement	standing charge/	adaptation	adjustment
	subscription	à debattre	negotiable
abonner	to subscribe	adoucisseur	water softener
abordable	affordable	d'eau	
aborder	to approach	aération	airing/ventilation
abords	surroundings	affaire	business/bargain
abri	shed/shelter	affaissement	subsidence
abrogation	abolition/annulment/	afférent	relating to
	cancellation	affermer	to lease
abus	abuse/breach	afficher	to advertise/post bills
abus de droit	misuse of law	agent immobilier	estate agent
abusif	abusive	agent locataire	letting agent
acajou	mahogany	agglomération	built-up area
accéder	to comply with	aggloméré	chipboard
acceptation	acceptance	agrandissement	extension
accès	access	aléatoire	contingent
accès pour	entrance for disabled	alimentaire	maintenance
handicapés		allant au four	oven proof
accessoires	ancillary/incidental	allée	path
accolée	semi-detached	amélioration	improvement
accord	agreement	aménagé	converted
accorder	to allow	ameublement	furniture
accrochage	fixing/hanging up	amovible	detachable/removable
accueil	reception/welcome	ampèrage	current
accumulateur	storage heater	ampoule	light bulb
acheminer	to channel	(électrique)	
acheter	to buy	annexe	extension
achèvement	completion	annuler	to cancel
acier	steel	antenne	aerial
acier inoxydable	stainless steel	antidérapant	non-skid
acompte	account/deposit/	appareil	domestic appliance
	instalment/	électroménager	
	down payment	appartement	apartment/flat
acoustique	acoustic	appartenir	to belong to
acquéreur	purchaser	appentis	lean-to
acquiescement	acceptance	applique	wall lamp

apprêter	to prime	augmenter	to increase
appui de fenêtre	windowsill (inside)	autocuiseur	pressure cooker
arbre	tree	autorisation	planning permission
arbuste	bush/shrub	(de construire)	
architecte paysagiste	landscape architect	auvent	awning/canopy
		avant-toit	eaves
architrave	architrave	avarie	damage
ardoise	slate	avenant	endorsement
are	100 square metres	avertissement	caveat/notice/warning
armature à toit	roof truss	aveu	acknowledgement/ admission
armoire	wardrobe		
arpenteur	surveyor	avis d'échéance	renewal notice
arrêt de façade	shutter fastening		
arrhes	deposit	bac de douche	shower tray
arrière-cuisine	scullery	bâche	tarpaulin
arrière-pays	back country	badigeon	distemper
arrondissement	borough/district	baguette	trim/beading/ cable cover
arrosage	watering		
arroseur	sprinkler	baignoire	bath
artisan	workman/craftsman	bail	lease/tenancy agreement
artisanat	handicraft		
artisan carreleur	ceramic tiler	bailleur	landlord
artisan maçon	builder	balcon	balcony
asbeste	asbestos	banc	bench
ascendant	parent, grandparent etc	bardeau	shingle
ascenseur	lift	barrière	gate/barrier
aspect mat	matt finish	barrière anti-humidité des remontées capillaires	damp-proof course
aspect velouté	silk finish		
aspect satiné	gloss finish		
asphalte	asphalt		
aspirateur	vacuum cleaner	bâtiment	building
assainissement	decontamination/ draining/purification	bâtir	to build
		bêche	spade
assemblages	joints	bédane	mortise chisel
assignation	citation/notice/service	benne	skip
assise	base	béton	concrete
assujetti	liable/taxpayer	béton armé	reinforced concrete
assurance	insurance	bétonnière	cement mixer
assurance de personnes	personal insurance	bibliothèque	bookcase
		bihebdomaire	bi-weekly
assurances dommages	property insurance	bimensuel	bi-weekly
		biseau	bevel
atelier	shop/workshop	bitume	bitumen
atermoiemont	delay	blocaille	hardcore
âtre	hearth/fireplace	bloc-évier	sink unit
attestation	certificate	bois	wood
auge	mixing trough	bois blanc	deal

bois de construction	timber	câble de distribution	mains cable
bois dur	hardwood	cadastre	town planning registry
boiserie	woodwork	cadenas	padlock
bois massif	solid wood	cadre	frame
boisseau	chimney flue tile	caduc	null
bois tendre	soft wood	cailloux	pebbles
boîte	box/garage	calfeutrage	draft proofing
boîte à ordures	rubbish bin	cambriolage	burglary
boîte aux lettres	letter/post box	camion	lorry
boîte de dérivation	junction box	canalisation	pipeline
		canapé	sofa
bord de mer	seaside	canapé-lit	sofa-bed
bord de rivière	riverside	caniveau	gutter
borne	terminal	caractéristique	feature
bouche d'aération	air vent	carelette	tile cutter
		carie	rot
bouleau	birch	carie sèche	dry rot
boulon	bolt	carillon	doorbell
bourrelet	beading/ draught excluder	carreau de faïence	ceramic tile
bouton de porte	door knob	carreau de liège	cork tile
bricoleur	handyman	carreau de plâtre	plaster board
brique	brick/building block	carrelet	square ruler
brique à air	air brick	carrelage	tiling
brique creuse	hollow brick	carrière	quarry
brique réfractaire	fire-proof brick	carte de commerçant	traders card
briquetage	brickwork	carte professionnelle	professional licence
brosse à maroufler	wallpaper brush	carton-cuir	hardboard
brosse d'encollage	pasting brush	cautionnement	guarantee
		cave	cellar
brosse métallique	wire brush	céder	to assign
		cèdre	cedar
brouette	wheelbarrow	centre des impôts	tax office
brouillon	draft		
broyeur à ordures	waste-disposal unit	certificat de conformité	building regulation approval
buanderie	utility room		
buffet	sideboard	certificat d'urbanisme	outline planning permission
buffet de cuisine	kitchen cabinet		
bureau des hypothêques	French land registry	cession	sale
		cession de bail	ssignment of a lease
butagaz	calor gas	CGI (Code Général des Impôts)	French tax law
cabinet	cabinet/office/ small room		
câble	cable	chalumeau	blow-lamp

chambranle	frame	ciseau de maçon	masonry chisel
chambre	room	citerne	water tank
chambre à coucher	bedroom	clapet	valve
Chambre de Commerce et d'Industrie	Chamber of Commerce	clef (à écrous)	spanner
		clés	keys
		clé à molette	adjustable spanner
Chambre des Métiers	Chamber of Trades	climatisation	air conditioning
		cloison	partition/dividing wall
chambre d'hôte	guest house	cloison contre l'humidité	damp proof course
chambre mansardée	loft conversion		
		clôture	fence/enclosure
champ	field	clou	nail
chantier de construction	building site	clou à béton	masonry nail
		clou cavalier	staple
chape	screed	clou de tapissier	carpet tack
charnière	hinge	Code Civil	French Civil Code
charpente	framework	Code de travail	French employment code
charpentier	carpenter		
chasse d'eau	flush toilet	coin	corner/wedge
châtaigne	chestnut	coin du feu	ingle-nook
chaudière	boiler	coin-cuisine	kitchenette
chaudière à gaz	gas fired boiler	colle	glue
chaudière à mazout	oil fired boiler	colocataires	co-tenants
		colombage	timber framed
chaudière à charbon	charcoal burning boiler	colonne	column
		comble	loft
chauffage	heating	commerçant	commercial trader
chauffage au mazout	oil fired heating	commode	chest of drawers
		commodités	lavatory
chauffage central	central heating	commun	common
		complémentaire	further/supplementary
chauffage sous-sol	under-floor heating	comporter	to include
		compromis de vente	contract
chauffe-eau	water heater		
chaume	thatch	comptable	accountant
chaumière	thatched cottage	comptabilité	book keeping
chemin	path	compte rendu	report
cheminée	chimney/fireplace	compte séquestre	stakeholder account
chêne	oak		
chéneau	gutter	compteur	meter
cheville	rawlplug	conception	design
chevron	rafter	concepteur	designer
ciment	cement	concierge	caretaker
ciseau à bois	wood chisel	condition suspensivea	condition precedent in contract
ciseau de briqueteur	brick/cold chisel		
		conduit	duct/shaft

conduit de cheminée	flue	coupe-circuit principal	main fuse
conduit de gaz	gas pipe	courant alternatif et continu	AC/DC
conduit d'évacuation	sewer	couteau universel	Stanley knife
conduite principale	water main	couvreur	roofer
		crampon	staple
congé	notice	crémone	rotating handle on shutters and windows
congédier	to dismiss		
congélateur	freezer	crèpe	stucco
conifère	conifer	crépi	rendering
conjoncteur	mains switch	crochet	door catch
conservatoire	conservatory	cuisine équippée	fitted kitchen
conserver	to retain	cuisinière	cooker
consignes en cas d'incendie	fire regulations	cuisinière à gaz	gas cooker
		cumulus électrique	immersion heater
constat	declaration of damage		
constat amiable	agreed accident report	cuvette	basin
constructeur	builder	cuvette de W C	toilet pan
construire	to build		
contemporain	contemporary	dallage	paving
contestation	dispute	dalle	flag/paving stone/ quarry tile
contourner	to by-pass/circumvent		
contrat	contract	dalles de miroir	mirror tiles
contrat d'assurances	insurance policy	débarras	box room
		débouchage des canalisations	unblocking the drains
contrat de travail	employment contract		
contravention	breach	décapant	paint stripper/scourer
contrecoeur	back-plate (of hearth)	déclaration annuelle	annual tax return
contremaître	foreman		
contre-plaqué	plywood	décolleuse	paper stripper
convecteur	convector heater	décompte	account/breakdown/ statement
convention d'occupation précaire	licence		
		dédommagement	compensation
		défaut d'entretien	maintenance failure
conversion	conversion	défaut de paiement	non payment
coordonnées téléphoniques	telephone number		
		défectueux	defective
corbeau	corbel	défonceuse	router
corniche	coving	défraîchi	faded
couche isolante	damp-proof course	dégager	to unblock
coude	plumbing bend	dégât	damage
coulage	substantial leak	dégorgement	discharge/overflow
coupe carreau	tile cutter	dégradations	degradation/erosion
coupe-circuit	fuse box	déhumidificateur	de-humidifier
coupe-circuit à fusible	fuse	déjeter	to warp
		délai	time limit

délayage	padding	double vitrage	double glazing
démarches	formalities	douche	shower
déménagement	removal	douchette	shower rose
demeure	residence	douille	lampholder/light switch
dépannage	fixing/repairing	draps	sheet
dépareillé	incomplete/spoilt	draps de bain	large towels
dépendance	outbuilding	dresser	to prepare
dépenses	maintenance expenses	droit	law/right/tax
d'entretien		droit de bail	tax on leases
dépôt de garantie	deposit	droit de passage	right of way
dépourvu	out of stock	droit de	pre-emption right
dérangement	inconvenience	préemption	
désaccord	dispute	droits de	French gifts tax
désagréments	disagreements	donation	
descriptif	descriptive/	droits de	French inheritance tax
	explanatory letter	succession	
dessécher	to dry out	duplex	duplex apartment/
désherbage	weeding		maisonette
désignation	description	durée	length/period
desservi	served/supplied		
dessin	drawing	eau	water
dessinateur	draftsman	eau de la ville	mains water
destination	permitted user	eau dure	hard water
des lieux		eau pluviale	rainwater
détartrer	to descale	eaux d'égout	sewage
détecteur	detector	ébauche	rough sketch
détendeur	gas pressure regulator	ébéniste	cabinet maker
déversoir	overflow	ébruiter	to leak out
devis	estimate	échafaud	scaffold
devis descriptif	bill of quantities	échantillon	cross section/sample
diamant	glass cutter	échéance	deadline/expiration
disjoncteur	trip switch/circuit	échelle	ladder/scale
	breaker	échelle d'incendie	fire escape
dispense	waiver	échelle double	step ladder
disponible	available	éclairage	lighting
dissimulation	concealment/evasion/	éclairage au	strip lighting
	witholding	néon	
divers	miscellaneous/sundry	écoulement	leak
dol	fraud	écrou	screw nut
doléance	grievance	écurie	stables
domaine	estate	EDF	French electricity
dommage	damage		company
dommages-	damages and interest	égout	sewer
intérêts		égout des toits	eaves
domicile	abode/home/residence	électrode	welding rod
domicile fiscal	tax residence	éléments	sanitary ware
double fenêtre	double glazing	sanitaire	

embaucher	to hire/employ	étayer	to shore up
empêchement	bar/disability/ obstruction	évacuation	waste water
		évier	sink
empiéter	to trespass	expert immobilier	surveyor
emplacement	location/site	expertise	survey
encadrement	framing	expiration du bail	termination of a lease
encaisser	to bank	extincteur	fire extinguisher
encastré	built-in	extracteur	extractor
enclos	paddock		
endommager	to damage	faire sauter les plombs	blow the fuses
enduit	plaster coating/ rendering/filler	fait des tiers	act of third parties
enfouchement	dovetailing	faïence	earthenwear
enlèvement	removal	faîte	ridge
enregistrement	registration of title	faîtière	ridge tile
en tontine	joint tenancy	fauteuil	armchair
entrebailleur à chaîne	security chain	faux plafond	false ceiling
		femme de ménage	cleaning lady
entremise	maintenance	fenêtre	window
entretenir	to maintain/upkeep/ service	fenêtre à battants	casement window
entretien	maintenance/upkeep	fenêtre à guillotine	sash window
enveloppe	cylinder jacket		
envelopper	to lag/wrap	fenêtre treillagée	lattice window
épaisseur	thickness	fer à souder	soldering iron
épave	wreck	fer forgé	wrought iron
épurateur	purifier	ferme	farm/fixed
équerre à dessin	set square	fermette	small farm
équerre droite	right angle	fermeture	catch/clasp/fastener
équipements communs	shared facilities	ferraillage	ironwork
		ferronnerie	ironwork
érable	maple	feutre à toit	roofing felt
escabeau	step ladder	fibres dures	hardboard
escalier	staircase	fibrociment	synthetic roof tiles
escalier de secours	fire escape	fil	cable
		fil à plomb	plumb-line
espagnolette	shutter/ window fastener	fil fusible	fuse wire
		filtre	filter
établi	work bench	finitions	finishing
étage	storey	fisc	tax authorities
étagère	shelves	fixer un prix	to quote
étanche	watertight	fléchir	to sag
étang	lake/pond	flotteur	ball cock
état des lieux	schedule of condition	foncier	to do with land/ property
état des lieux de sortie	schedule of dilapidation	fonctionnement	operation/running
état moyen	average condition	fondation	foundation

fonds de commerce	business assets	gercement	chapping/cracking
fonds de clientèle	goodwill	gestation	management
fongible	soft	glace	ice
fongicide	fungicide	gond	shutter hinge pin
fonte	cast iron	goudron	tar
force majeure	act of God	goulet d'étranglement	bottleneck
foret	drill	gouttière	gutter
forêt	forest	graissage	greasing/lubricating
foret pour le métal	metal drill	grandeur	size
		grange	barn
forfaitaire	fixed (amount)	graphique	chart/diagram/graph
forte agrafeuse	staple gun	grattoir	scraper
fossé	ditch/gulf/cap	gravier	gravel
fosse d'aisance	cesspool	gravillons	loose chippings
fosse septique	septic tank	grêle	hail
four	oven	grenier	attic/loft/barn
four à micro-ondes	microwave oven	grès	sandstone
		griffe	tile scorer
fourneau à gaz	gas heater	gril	grill
fournisseur	supplier	grillage	wire netting/mesh
foyer	hearth/fireplace	grille	gate/window grill
fraise	countersink		
frêne	ash (wood)	habileté	craft/expertise
frigidaire	fridge	habitation	dwelling
front de mer	seashore	hache	axe
fuite	leak	haie	hedge
fusible	fuse	hameau	hamlet
fusible à cartouche	cartridge fuse	hangar	Dutch/open barn
		hauteur libre	headroom
frigo	fridge	hebdomodaire	weekly
		hébergement	accommodation/lodging
gâche	catch of a lock		
gaine	sheathing	hectare	2.2 acres
galvaniser	to galvanise	héritier	heir/beneficiary
garde-corps	railings	hêtre	beech
garde-feu	fire guard	heures creuses	off-peak
garde-robe	wardrobe	honoraires	fees
gardien	caretaker	horloge	clock (large)
garniture	upholstery	HT (hors taxe)	exclusive of tax
gaz	gas	hors-cote	kerbstone
gaz de ville	mains gas	hors saison	out of season
gazon	turf/lawn	housse	cover
GDF	French gas company	huile	oil
gel	frost	huile de lin	linseed oil
géomètre expert	land surveyor	humidificateur	humidifier
gérant	manager	humidité	damp

huissier de justice	bailiff/process server	inter horaire	time switch
hypothèque	mortgage	intérimaire	interim/temporary
		intermédiaire	agent/intermediary
		interphone	entry phone/intercom
if	yew	interrupteur	on/off switch
immatriculation	registration	interrupteur va-et-vient	two-way switch
immeubles	buildings		
imperméable	waterproof	interurbain	intercity
imposable	taxable	intimité	privacy
imposte	fanlight	intituler	to entitle
impôt	tax	inventaire	inventory
impôt de solidarité sur la fortune (ISF)	wealth tax	isolant	insulating
		isolation (phonique/ acoustique/ thermal)	sound/heat insulation
impôt sur les plus values	capital gains tax		
impôt sur le revenu des personnes physiques (IRPP)	income tax	isolé	isolated
		jalon	landmark/milestone
		jalousie	slatted blind
impôt sur les sociétés (IS)	corporation tax	jardin de rocaille	rock garden
		jardinière	window box
imputation	charge/imputation	jauge	guage
imprévu	contingency	jauge à mazout	fuel guage
improvisé	makeshift	jeu de clès	set of spanners
incendie	arson/fire	joint	grouting
indemnité	indemnity/ compensation	joint d'étanchéité	draft excluder
		jointoyer	point brickwork
indemnité d'éviction	compensation for eviction	jouissance	enjoyment/ possession
indivis	undivided	jumelée	semi-detached
indivision	joint ownership	jumelle	semi-detached
inexécution	breach		
infiltration	seepage/rising damp	lâche	loose
ingénieur	engineer	laque	lacquer
inhabité	uninhabited	laine d'acier	wire wool
inondation	flood	laine de verre	fibreglass
inox	stainless steel	laiton	brass
inoxydable	rustproof	lambrequin	pelmet
inscription	registration	lambris	cladding/tongue and groove panelling
insidieux	creeping		
insonorisation	sound proofing	lampe à souder à gaz	blow lamp
installation	fittings		
installation téléphonique	telephone	lampe de table	table lamp
		largeur	width
insuffisance	deficiency	latte	batten
interdiction	ban/prohibition	latté	blockboard

lattis	lathwork	machine à laver	washing machine
lavabo	washbasin	maçon	builder/bricklayer
lave-mains	hand basin	maçonnerie	masonry
laverie	laundry	magnétoscope	video recorder
laveur de carreaux	window cleaner	maillet	mallet
		main courante	handrail/bannister
lave-vaisselle	dishwasher	mains d'oeuvre	labour/manpower/ workforce
lézarde	crack		
libérer	to vacate	maintien	maintenance
liège	cork tiling	maire	mayor
lien	attachment/link/tie	mairie	town hall
limites de terrain	boundary	maison	house
lingerie	linen room	maison d'amis	weekend house
linteau	lintel	maison de campagne	country house
lit	bed		
lit bateau	antique bed	maison de maître	gentleman's house
lit de traverse	alcove bed	maison jumelle	semi detached house
literie	bedding	maison mère	parent company
littoral	coast	maison paysanne	farm-house
living	living room		
livrable	available	maisonette	cottage
livraison	delivery	majoration	increase/rise/surcharge
livrer	to deliver	malfaçon	defect/fault
local	community/parish	manchon	sleeve/ straight coupling
locataire	tenant		
location	hire/letting	mandat	Power of Attorney/ proxy
location meublée	furnished letting		
location saisonnière	holiday let	mandat de recherche	power given to someone to find a property
locaux vacants	vacant premises		
logement	accommodation/ dwelling	mandataire	authorised agent
		manoir	manor
longueur	length	manteau de cheminée	chimney piece
loquet	latch		
loqueteau	door catch/small hinge	marbre	marble
lotissement	housing estate	marche	step
louer	to hire/let	marquise	porch
loué	let	marteau	hammer
loyer	rent	marteau à deux mains	sledge hammer
lucarne	dormer window/ skylight		
		marteau de démolition	mechanical hammer
lu et approuvé	read and approved		
lumière	light/electric light	marteau d'emballeur	claw hammer
lumière de chevet	bedside lamp		
		mas	farmhouse
lumineux	luminous	mastic	putty/filler
lustre	gloss	matelas	mattress

matelas à ressorts	spring mattress	motopompe	power-driven pump
		moulure	moulding
matériaux de construction	building material	mousse	moss
		multirisque	multi-risk
mat	matt	municipal	borough/civic council
mazout	fuel oil	mur	wall
mèche à bois/ à beton	wood/concrete drill/bit	mur de clèture	boundary wall
		mur mitoyen	party wall
mélangeur	mixer tap	murs extérieurs	exterior walls
mélèze	larch	muret	low wall
mensuel	monthly	muret en pierre sèche	dry stone wall
menuiserie	joinery		
menuisier	joiner		
menus entretiens	minor repairs	nappe	expanse/layer/sheet
menus réparations	minor repairs	nettoyage	cleaning
		nettoyant	cleaning fluid
menuiserie	woodwork	neutre	neutral
mètre carré	square metre	niveau	level/grade
mètre pliant	folding rule	niveau à bulle d'air	spirit level
mètre ruban	tape measure		
metreur	quantity surveyor	noix	walnut
metreur vérificateur	quantity surveyor	nommer	to appoint
		non-goudronné	unmade (road)
mettre à terre	to earth	non-livraison	non-delivery
meublé	furnished	non-meublé	unfurnished
meuble à demeure	fitment	normes	standards
		note de renseignements d'urbanisime	local authority search
meubles	furniture		
meublés classés tourisme	classified tourist accommodation		
		notaire	notary
milieu	environment/middle	notification	notice
minuterie	time-switch		
miroir	mirror	occasion	second hand
mise en demeure	notice	occultation	overshadowing
mitigeurs	mixer tap	occuper	to occupy
mitoyen	intermediate	odeur	smell
moellons	rubble/quarry stone	oeuvre	work
mobilier	furnishings	oléoduc	pipeline
mois	month	omettre	to omit
moisissure	fungus/mildew	opaque	opaque
moquette	fitted carpet	ordinateur	computer
morceler	to break up/partition	ordures	rubbish
mortier	mortar/grout	oreiller	pillow
mortier colle	tile cement	oriel	bow/bay window
mortier rapide	quick setting cement	orme	elm
mortier réfractaire	heat resistant cement	ortie	nettle
mosaïque	mosaic	outil	tool

outillage	equipment/machinery	peinture laquée	enamel
outre	in addition to	pelle	shovel
ouverture	opening	pelouse	lawn
ouvrier	workman	pendule	clock (small)
ouvrier maçon	bricklayer	pépinière	garden centre
		perceuse	drill
paiement comptant	cash payment	périmé	out of date
		permis de construire	planning permission
paillasson	door mat		
paisiblement	peacefully	persienne	blind/slatted shutter
pallier	landing	personne physique	individual
pâlir	to fade		
palissandre	rosewood	personne morale	company
paillasson d'entrée	doormat	perte	loss
		peuplier	poplar
panne	breakdown	phase	phase (electrical)
papier de verre	sandpaper	pièce	room (kitchen and bathroom not counted)
papier peint	wallpaper		
papier préencollé	ready pasted wallpaper		
		pied-de-biche	claw hammer
parcelle	allotment/lot/parcel	pin	pine
parking	parking lot	pierre	stone
parois	partition walls	pierre concassée	crushed stone
paroisse	parish	pignon	gable
parpaing	breeze block	pilier	pillar
parquet	parquet	pinceau	paintbrush
partager	to share/split	pinces	pliers
parterre	flower bed	pioche	pickaxe
particulier	individual	pipe à sortir	evacuation pipe
parties communes	common parts of a building	piquet de terre	earthing pin
		piscine	swimming pool
parties privatives	private parts of a building	pistolet	spray gun
		placage	veneer
passe-plat	service hatch	placard	built-in cabinet/cupboard/veneer
paumelle	split hinge		
pavage	pavement	place de stationnement	parking space
pavé	paving stone		
pavillon	summer house	placoplâtre	plasterboard
peindre et tapisser	to decorate	plafond	ceiling/cap
		plain-pied	single storey
peine	penalty/sanction/sentence	plan	chart/plan
		planche	plank/floorboard
peintre	painter	planche d'échafaudage	scaffold board
peinture	paint/painting		
peinture acrylique	acrylic paint	planchéiage	boarding
peinture crépi	masonry paint	plancher	floor boards
peinture émulsion	emulsion paint	plan	plan

plaque chauffante	hob/hot plate	poutre	beam
plaque d'égout	manhole cover	poutres apparentes	exposed beams
platane	plain tree		
plateau	shelf	poutrelle	small beam
plate-bande	flower bed	pouvoir	power
plâtre	plaster	préavis	notice
plâtrier	plasterer	préjudice	damage
plâtroir	plastering trowel	prélèvement automatique	standing order
plinthe	skirting board		
plomb	lead	premier étage	first floor
plomberie	plumbing	preneur	tenant
plombier	plumber	prénom	first name
plus-value	capital gain	prime	premium
poêle	wood-burning stove	prise	electric socket/ power point
poignée	handle		
poignée de porte	door handle	prise de terre	earthing point/socket
poinçon	awl/bradawl	prix fixé	fixed price
police	police/policy	procuration	power of attorney
polyvalant	multi-purpose	profondeur	depth
pompe	pump	projecteur	floodlight
pompe de puisard	sump	projet	draft
		prolongateur	extension lead
pompiers	fire brigade	promoteur immobilier	property developer
ponceuse	sander		
ponceuse à bande	belt sander	promesse de vente	contract
ponceuse vibrante	orbital sander	propre	clean
		propriétaire	owner
porche	porch	propriété	property
portail	garden gate/gateway	province	country (as opposed to town)
porte	door/gate		
porte coulissante	sliding door	provisoire	draft/interim/ provisional/temporary
porte va-et-vient	swing door		
porte-fenêtre	French window	proximité	near/proximity
porte-blindée	reinforced door	puisard	cesspool/sink/sump
porte fusible	fuse box	puissance	capacity/power/ strength/wattage
porte vitre	glass door		
portillon	gate	puits	well
pose	fix	puits perdu	soakaway
pose des vitres	glazing	purger	to clear
poste de soudage à l'arc	arc welder	pylône	pylon
pot de cheminée	chimney pot	quartier	quarter
potager	kitchen garden	queue-d'aronde	dovetail
poubelle	dustbin	quincaillerie	hardware/ironmongery
poulie	pulley	quinzaine	fortnight
pourrissement	rot	quittance	receipt

quitus	discharge	réglage de la temperature	temperature control
quote-part	contribution		
quotidien	daily	règle	rule/ruler
		règle niveau	spirit level
rabot	plane	règlement	payment/settlement
raccord	joint/connection	règlement de copropriété	lease of the common parts
raccord coudé	bend joint		
raclette	scraper	réglet métallique	metal knife
radiateur soufflant	fan heater	remblai	ballast/embankment/ hardcore
rainure et longuette	tongue and groove	remis à neuf	replacement as new
		remise	garage/shed/store
rallonge	extension	remise des clefs	handing over of keys
ramonage	chimney sweeping	renforcer	to reinforce/strengthen
ramoneur	chimney sweep	renonciation	abandonment/ renunciation
rampants	roof arches		
rampe d'escalier	bannister	renouveler	to renew
		rénové	renovated
rangements	storage space	renseignements	enquiries/information
râpe	rasp	réparation	repair
rapport d'avant projet	feasibility report	répertoire des métiers	trade register
rapport d'expertise	loss adjuster's report	replâtrage	patching up
		représentant	representative
ravalement	cleaning/restoration	résilier	to cancel/terminate
rayer	to scratch	responsabilité civile	civil liability
raz de marée	landslide		
reboisement	reafforestation	resserrer	to squeeze/lighten
rebord de fenêtre	window-sill (inside)	restauration	restoration
		restaurer	to restore
réception des travaux	completion of building works	restitution des clés	return of the keys
réclamation	claim	rétrécir	to narrow
recoin	recess	revêtement	new coating or facing surface
reconduction	renewal		
rectifier	to amend	revêtement de sol	floor covering
reçu	receipt		
rédaction	preparing/drafting	rez-de-chaussée	ground floor
redevable	taxpayer	rideau	curtain
redevance	due/fee/tax	risque	hazard/risk
refait	restored	ristourne	drawback
réfectoire	dining room	rive de toits	roof edge
regard de visite	inspection chamber	riverain	riperian/bordering
Registre du Commerce et des Sociétés (RCS)	companies registry	robinet	tap
		robinet de fermeture	stop cock
		robinet de purge	air release tap

robinet thermostatique	thermostatic radiator tap
robinetterie	plumbing/taps
rondelle	washer
rosace	ceiling rose
rètissoire	spit
rouille	rust
rouleau à peinture	paint roller
rubrique	column/heading
ruine	run-down property
ruisseau	stream
rupture	breach
SA	corporation
sablager	to sandblast
sable	sand
sable doux	soft sand
salle à manger	dining room
salle de bain	bathroom
salle de séjour	living room
salon	living room/lounge
sanitaire	sanitary
sans cloisons	open plan
sans effet	void
sans littoral	landlocked
SARL	limited liability company
sapin	fir
saule	willow
sellé	padlock/seal
SCI	non-trading property holding company
scie	saw
scie à chaînette	chainsaw
scie à métaux	hacksaw
scie à chantourner	jig saw
scie à ruban	band saw
scie à tenon	tenon saw
scie circulaire	circular saw
scie mécanique	circular saw
scie sans fin	band saw
scie sauteuse	jig saw
scie vilebrequin	ceramic tile cutting saw
seau	bucket
sèche-linge	clothes dryer
séjour	living room/stay
semaine	week
semelle	roofplate
semestriel	bi-yearly
se prendre en glace	freeze up
séquoia	redwood
serre	conservatory/glasshouse
serrure	lock
serrurier	locksmith
service d'eau	water authority
service de ménage	cleaning services
services collectifs	collective services
seuil	sill/threshold
siège	seat/registered office
siège pour bébé	baby chair
signal d'incendie	fire alarm
siphon	water/drain tap
société	company
socle	insulating base
sol	ground/floor
solidaire	joint
solidairement	jointly and severally
solive	joist
sommation	notice
somme garantie	sum insured
sonnette	door bell
sonnerie d'alarme	alarm bell/burglar alarm
souder	to weld
soudure	solder
soupape	valve
sous-couche	undercoat
sous-location	sublease
sous-louer	to sublet
sous seing privé	legal document not registered with a notaire
sous-sol	basement/underground
soussigné	undersigned
sous-traitance	subcontracting
station d'épuration	purification plant
statuts	memorandum and articles of association

store	roller blind	toile de jute	hessian
store vénitien	venetian blind	toit	roof
succession	estate for inheritance purposes	toit en ardoise	slate roof
		toiture	roofing
superficie	acreage/area/surface	tôle ondulée	corrugated iron
support	prop/bearer	tondeuse	lawn mower
surpeuplement	overpopulation	tontine	joint tenancy
surplomb	overhang	tournevis	screwdriver
syndic	managing agent of a block of flats	tout à l'égout	mains drainage
		travailleur indépendant	self-employed person
table à encoller	pasting table	travaux d'amélioration	improvement/ renovation works
table de toilette	dressing table		
table de nuit	bedside table	travaux publics	public works
tablette	shelf	travaux temporaires	temporary works
tablette de cheminée	mantelpiece		
		treillage	trellis work
tabouret	stool	treillis métallique	wire netting
tacite reconduction	tacit renewal	treillis soudé	welded steel mesh
		tréteau	trestle
taille	size	trimestre	quarter (three months)
tapis	rug/carpet	tronçonneuse	chain saw
targette	bolt	trop-plein	waste pipe
tasseau	bracket	trou	hole/air vent
taudis	slum	trou de serrure	keyhole
taxe d'habitation	residential tax	trou de sondage	bore hole
taxes foncières	land and building taxes	trou de vers	worm hole
taxe professionnelle	business tax	trou de visite	manhole
		truelle	trowel
taxe de séjour	tax on hotel accommodation	truelle de maçon	masonry trowel
		trumeau	chimney breast
teck	teak	tube de cuivre	copper pipe
tenon et mortaise	mortise and tenon	tuile	roof tile
tension du courant	voltage	tuile de rive	edge tile
		tuyau	tube/pipe
terrain	field/ground/land	tuyau d'arrosage	hosepipe
terrain à bâtir	building plot	tuyau d'écoulement	drain pipe
terre	earth		
terre cuite	unglazed brick/ terracotta	tuyau de descente	down pipe
		tuyau d'égout	soil pipe
testament	will	tuyau de vidange	drain pipe
textile muraux	fabric wall covering	tuyauterie	piping
tilleul	lime tree	tuyau en PVC	PVC pipe
tiroir	drawer	TVA	VAT
tissu	fabric/cloth		
tissus d'ameublement	furnishing fabrics	urbanisme	town planning

usine	factory	vice de construction	defect in construction
ustensiles	utensils	vidange	draining
usufruit	life interest	vide-ordures	rubbish bin
usufruitier	life tenant	vilebrequin	bit brace
usure	wear and tear	villa	detached house
		virement	bank transfer
vaisselle	crockery/dishes	vis	screw
valeur à neuf	value as new	vis à calotte	mirror screw
valeur de remplacement	replacement value	vis à tête fraisée	countersunk screw
		vis à tête ronde	dome headed screw
variateur	dimmer switch	visite des lieux	site inspection
velours	velvet	visser	to screw on
vente	sale	vitrage	glazing
verger	orchard	vitre	glass/window pane
vermoulu	worm-eaten	vitrier	glazer
vernis	varnish	vitrification	glazing
verre	glass	voie privée	driveway
verre à pied	stemmed glass	voisin	neighbour
verrou	bolt	volet	shutter
vers à bois	woodworm	volige	thin plank
vestibule	entrance hall	voûte	vault
vétusté	wear and tear	voyant	garish/gaudy/loud
vétusté deduite	deduction for wear and tear		
viabilisé	building site on which the roads have been made	watt	watt
		white-spirit	white spirit
vice	defect/flaw	zinc	zinc
vices cachés	hidden defects	zone	area/zone